PSALMS

Beyond 2000

Fr. Bommarito

May God bless you —

Mark Smith

PSALMS

Beyond 2000

A PRAYER JOURNEY

MARK LINK

ThomasMore®

ALLEN, TEXAS

IMPRIMI POTEST
Bradley M. Schaeffer, S.J.

NIHIL OBSTAT
Rev. Msgr. Glenn D. Gardner, J.C.D.
Censor Librorum

IMPRIMATUR
† Most Rev. Charles V. Grahmann
Bishop of Dallas

October 4, 1996

The Nihil Obstat and Imprimatur are official declarations
that the material reviewed is free of doctrinal or moral
error. No implication is contained therein that those
granting the Nihil Obstat and Imprimatur agree with the
contents, opinions, or statements expressed.

ACKNOWLEDGMENT

Unless otherwise noted, all Scripture quotations are
from Today's English Version text. Copyright © American
Bible Society 1966, 1971, 1976, 1992. Used by permission.

Cover photo: Dennis Junor/Superstock

Psalms Beyond 2000 is the expanded journal edition
of *Psalms 2000*.

Send all inquiries to:
Thomas More® Publishing
200 East Bethany Drive
Allen, Texas 75002-3804

Toll Free   800-264-0368
Fax   800-688-8356

Printed in the United States of America

ISBN 0-88347-360-7

1 2 3 4 5   00 99 98 97 96

Contents

▼II The Psalms and Jesus   170

How to Use *Psalms Beyond 2000*

There are two ways to use this book:

- on your own or
- as a member of a support group.

If you pray it on your own,
simply devote ten minutes a day
to each meditation exercise.

If you pray it as a member of a group,
you also meet with six to eight friends
once a week.

Guidelines for Meditating Daily

Begin each daily meditation by praying
the following prayer reverently:

Father, you created me
and put me on earth for a purpose.
Jesus, you died for me
and called me to complete your work.
Holy Spirit, you help me
to carry out the work
for which I was created and called.
In your presence and name—
Father, Son, and Spirit—
I begin my meditation.
May all my thoughts and inspirations
have their origin in you
and be directed to your glory.

The format for each meditation
is as follows:

- *Read* the meditation exercise slowly.
  When you finish, return to any
  phrase, sentence, or idea
  that struck you while reading.
  (Spend about one minute on this step.)

- *Think* about the phrase, sentence,
  or idea that struck you.
  Why did it strike you?
  (Spend about four minutes on this step.)

- *Speak* to God about your thoughts.
  Talk to God as you would to a close
  and trusted friend.
  (Spend about one minute on this step.)

- *Listen* to God's response.
  What may God wish to say to you?
  (Spend about four minutes on this step.)

End each meditation by reciting
the Lord's Prayer slowly and reverently.
Then jot down in the journal space
whatever struck you most
during your meditation.

N.B: The "Daily Meditation Format,"
including the opening meditation prayer,
is printed on page 12.

Guidelines for Meeting Weekly

The purpose of the weekly meeting
is for *support* and *sharing*.
Meetings are thirty to forty minutes long,
unless the group decides otherwise.
The meeting starts with a "Call to Prayer."
A member lights a candle and
the following prayer is said reverently:

FIRST READER
  [Jesus said,]
  "I am the light of the world. . . .
  Whoever follows me
  will have the light of life
  and will never walk in darkness." John 8:12

SECOND READER
  Lord Jesus, you also said
  that where two or three
  come together in your name,
  you are there with them.
  The light of this candle
  symbolizes your presence among us.

THIRD READER
  And, Lord Jesus,
  where you are, there too
  are the Father and the Spirit.
  And so we begin our meeting
  in the presence and the name
  of the Father,
  the Son,
  and the Holy Spirit.

The meeting proper begins
with the leader responding briefly
to these two questions:

1. How faithful was I to my commitment
   to reflect daily on the Bible reading?
2. Which daily meditation
   was most meaningful for me and why?

The leader then invites each member,
in turn, to respond briefly
to the same two questions.
When all have responded,
the leader opens the floor
to anyone who wishes

- to elaborate on his or her response
  to the second question or
- to comment on another's response
  (not to take issue with it,
  but to affirm or clarify it).

The meeting ends
with a "Call to Mission":
a charge to witness to Jesus and
to his teaching in daily life.
It consists
in reverently praying the following:

FIRST READER
We conclude our meeting
by listening to Jesus say to us
what he said to his disciples
in his Sermon on the Mount:

SECOND READER
"You are like light for the whole world.
A city built on a hill cannot be hid.
No one lights a lamp
and puts it under a bowl;
instead it is put on the lampstand,
where it gives light
for everyone in the house.
In the same way
your light must shine before people,
so that they will see the good things
you do and praise your Father in heaven."
Matthew 5:14–16

Then a member extinguishes the candle
(lit at the start of the meeting).

FINAL READER
The light of this candle
is now extinguished.
But the light of Christ in each of us
must continue to shine in our lives.
Toward this end
we pray together the Lord's Prayer:
"Our Father . . ."

For handy reference the "Call to Prayer"
and the "Call to Mission" are printed
on pages 12–13.

Daily Meditation Format

Begin each meditation with this prayer:

Father, you created me
and put me on earth for a purpose.
Jesus, you died for me
and called me to complete your work.
Holy Spirit, you help me
to carry out the work
for which I was created and called.
In your presence and name—
Father, Son, and Holy Spirit—
I begin my meditation.
May all my thoughts and inspirations
have their origin in you
and be directed to your glory.

Follow this format for each meditation:

1. READ the meditation prayerfully.
   (About one minute.)
2. THINK about what struck you most
   as you read the meditation. Why this?
   (About four minutes.)
3. SPEAK to God about your thoughts.
   (About one minute.)
4. LISTEN to God's response.
   Simply rest in God's presence
   with an open mind and an open heart.
   (About four minutes.)
5. END each meditation by praying the
   Lord's Prayer slowly and reverently.

Weekly Meeting Format

CALL TO PRAYER

*The leader begins each weekly meeting
by having someone light a candle
and then reading the following prayerfully:*

Jesus said,
"I am the light of the world. . . .
Whoever follows me
will have the light of life
and will never walk in darkness."
                                        John 8:12

Lord Jesus, you also said
that where two or three
come together in your name,
you are there with them.
The light of this candle
symbolizes your presence among us.

And, Lord Jesus,
where you are,
there, too,
are the Father and the Holy Spirit.
So we begin our meeting
in the presence and the name
of the Father,
the Son,
and the Holy Spirit.

Weekly Meeting Format

CALL TO MISSION

> *The leader ends each weekly meeting*
> *by reading the following prayerfully:*

We conclude our meeting
by listening to Jesus say to us
what he said to his disciples
in his Sermon on the Mount:

"You are like light for the whole world.
A city built on a hill cannot be hid.
No one lights a lamp
and puts it under a bowl;
instead it is put on the lampstand,
where it gives light
for everyone in the house.
In the same way
your light must shine before people,
so that they will see
the good things you do
and praise your Father in heaven."

Matthew 5:14–16

> *A member extinguishes the candle.*
> *Then the leader continues:*

The light of this candle
is now extinguished.
But the light of Christ in each of us
must continue to shine in our lives.
Toward this end we pray together
the Lord's Prayer: "Our Father . . ."

Timelessness of the Psalms

Symphony conductor Guy Harrison
had a notebook in which he summarized
every book he had read.
He said that those notes allowed him
"to recapture the spirit and substance
of each book."

What Harrison's notebook did for him,
the Book of Psalms did for Israel.
It summarized in prayer and song
the "spirit and substance"
of the Old Testament.
This explains why Old Testament readings
in many worship services
are followed by the reading of a psalm.
Called a responsorial psalm,
it acts as a prayerful response
to the reading.

This brings us to an important point.
The psalms deal with basic spiritual issues
and therefore transcend time.
An example will illustrate.

Years ago a New Mexico hot-air balloonist,
Kathleen Baker-Gumprecht,
ran into a serious problem in a stretch
of desert outside of Albuquerque.

In the midst of her harrowing experience,
she found herself praying a psalm
that she had memorized as a child:

"Call to me when trouble comes;
I will save you,
and you will praise me." Psalm 50:15

She said, "Suddenly I knew I wasn't alone.
I felt calm. Strength poured through me."
Fifteen minutes later,
she was on the ground, safe and sound.

That day Kathleen discovered what so many
other Christians have over the centuries:
the psalms are timeless prayers.
They are as relevant today as they were
when David prayed them in the desert,
or when Mary probably prayed them
while working around the house in Nazareth.

It is to those same psalms
that we now turn.

A psalm
is a cry of happiness,
the echo of gladness.

It soothes the temper,
lightens the sorrow.
It is a source of security by night,
a lesson of wisdom by day.

It is
a shield when we are afraid,
a celebration of holiness,
a vision of serenity,
a promise of peace and harmony.

Day begins to the music of a psalm.
Day closes to the echo of a psalm.

Saint Ambrose (4th century)

The Lord said . . . ,
"Write an account of this . . . ,
so that it will be remembered."
Exodus 17:14

Prayer Journal–1

Someone once said,
"I had gotten so caught up in my work
that I had not meditated for two weeks.
I didn't intend to stop; it just happened.
Then, while looking for something else,
I noticed my prayer journal.
I stopped to read from it.
This started me meditating again."

A prayer journal is simply a brief record
of a thought, feeling, or idea
that occurred during my meditation.
I might address it directly to God.

For example, I might write:
"Lord, thank you for helping me see
that 'what I am' is your gift to me
and 'what I become' is my gift back to you."*

This week I will record
in the "journal" space provided
a brief entry concerning
each of my daily meditations,
addressing it directly to God.

---

* Instructions throughout this book are written in the first person to invite the
 reader to enter more fully into the process of meditating on the Psalms.

O God, happy are they who do your will.

Journal

The play *The Teahouse of the August Moon*
opens with Sakini all alone on stage.
He is an interpreter for the American army
on the island of Okinawa.
Sakini wears ill-fitting clothes
and his GI shoes are several sizes too big.
He moves slowly to the footlights,
bows to the audience,
and introduces the play.
The Book of Psalms begins in a similar way.
The psalmist walks to the footlights,
bows to the reader—as it were—and says:

Happy are those . . .
who do not follow the example of sinners. . . .
They are like trees . . .
that bear fruit at the right time. . . .
But evil people are not like this . . . ;
they are like straw
that the wind blows away. . . .
The righteous are . . . protected by the LORD,
but the evil are on the way to their doom.   1, 3–4, 6

Jesus probably had this passage in mind
when he said, "A tree is known by the kind
of fruit it bears" (Matthew 12:33).
What would I say if Jesus asked me right now,
"What type of fruit are you bearing?"

It's easy to make a buck; it's tougher
to make a difference.   Tom Brokaw at Notre Dame

17

Journal

O God, foolish are they who oppose your will.

Israel's kings were religious figures
as well as political figures. Their coronation
made them God's "son" in a special sense.
To plot against them was to plot against God.
It was sheer folly.
Moreover, the coronation of a new king
brought Israel a step closer
to the "King of Kings," the promised Messiah,
Jesus, the "Son of God."
And so when Herod and Pilate plotted
to kill Jesus, Christians applied Psalm 2
to these two leaders (Acts 4:25–27).

Why do the nations plan rebellion? . . .
Their rulers plot together against the LORD
and against the king. . . .
From his throne in heaven the Lord laughs
and mocks their feeble plans. . . . [He says,]
"I have installed my king . . . my son;
today I have become your father. . . ."
Now listen to this warning . . .
you rulers of the world: Serve the LORD . . .
or else his anger will be quickly aroused.
1–2, 4, 6–7, 10–11

How am I serving the Lord? What am I doing
to bring God's kingdom to completion?

Lord, here I am.
What would you have me to do?
Saint Francis Xavier

O God, you give me victory and restore my courage.

Journal

Martin Gray grew up when an infamous wall
was erected to imprison the Jews
of a Warsaw ghetto. Later, at Treblinka,
he helped carry bodies to mass graves.
Martin describes all these things in his book
For Those I Loved. It's a moving story
of how he tried to convince himself, at first,
that these things were not really happening.
In the course of it he makes a disturbing point:
the Nazis were not the only beasts;
the people who looked the other way
were also beasts in their own way.
The Jewish victim of Martin's time
could relate to these words of the psalmist:

I have so many enemies, Lord,
so many who turn against me!
They talk about me and say,
"God will not help him." . . .
Come, Lord! Save me, my God! . . .
Victory comes from the Lord—
may he bless his people.   1–2, 7–8

What is one evil in today's world
that disturbs and pains me?
What is one thing I might do to combat it?

It is the greatest of all mistakes
to do nothing
because you can only do a little.
Do what you can.   Sydney Smith

19

Journal

You have blessed me, O God, with joy and peace.

Babe Ruth was in a New York hospital,
facing a serious operation.
Paul Carey, one of Ruth's closest friends,
was at his bedside.
Paul said to the Babe, "Don't you think
you ought to put your house in order?"
Ruth wrote later:
"For the first time I realized that death
might strike me out. I nodded,
and Paul got up, called in a chaplain,
and I made a full confession. . . .
As I lay in bed that evening I thought
to myself what a comfortable feeling
to be free from fear and worries.
I now could simply turn them over to God."
The Guideposts Treasury of Faith
The psalmist recounts a similar peace:

There are many who pray:
"Give us more blessings, O LORD.
Look on us with kindness!"
But the joy that you have given me
is more than they will ever have. . . .
I go to sleep in peace; you alone,
O LORD, keep me perfectly safe. 6–8

When did I feel the kind of peace
that Ruth and the psalmist speak of?

Lord, make me an instrument of your peace.
Saint Francis of Assisi

Hear my words, O God, and heed my sighs.

An old poem concerns a preacher
who draws great crowds.
Each time he preaches,
an old brother sits upon the pulpit steps
and pleads with God to "stir the souls"
and "melt the hearts" of all who hear.
One night the monk is alone in the church,
rejoicing that God has blessed him
with such great ability.
Suddenly an angel speaks, "Oh no, my son!
Souls are stirred and hearts are melted
not by your great preaching ability
but by the brother's heartfelt pleading
as he sits upon the pulpit steps and prays."

Listen to my words, O LORD,
and hear my sighs. . . .
I pray to you, O LORD;
you hear my voice in the morning;
at sunrise I offer my prayer.   1–3

How convinced am I that prayer
puts a mighty power into my hands?
What keeps me from using this power
as the brother did?

More things are wrought by prayer
Than this world dreams of.
Wherefore, let thy voice
Rise like a fountain day and night.
Alfred Lord Tennyson, *Morte d'Arthur*

Journal

21

Journal

Have pity on me, O God, and come to my rescue.

Lecturer David Hubbard
was on a ship en route to England.
His cabin was extremely tiny and dark.
The fourth night at sea,
he awoke with a jolt, gasping for air.
The cabin walls seemed to close in on him.
Anxiety and panic engulfed him.
It was then that he turned to God
in a way that he had never done before.
He asked God to reach down from heaven,
give him strength, and fill him with calm.
God did!
Hubbard said the experience of that night
gave him a new appreciation of Psalm 6.

I am worn out, O LORD; have pity on me!
Give me strength; I am completely exhausted
and my whole being is deeply troubled.
How long, O LORD, will you wait to help me?
Come and save me, LORD;
in your mercy rescue me from death.   2–4

When did I feel the need for God's help
with every fiber of my being?

We shall steer safely through every storm,
so long as our heart is right,
our intention fervent,
our courage steadfast,
and our trust fixed firmly on God.
Saint Francis de Sales

I thank you, O God, and sing your praises.

A college student
went to a convenience store late at night.
A gang member whose initiation demanded
that he steal the ID of a college student
hit him on the head with a rock.
For weeks the student
hovered precariously between life and death.
Miraculously he recovered but had problems
accepting lingering effects of the injury.
He joined a head-injury therapy group
and was counseled to treat his "injury day"
as his "new birthday."
This counsel taught him an important truth.
Peace of mind and health lay not in anger
at being injured but in surrender to God,
who can draw good from evil.
The student could now pray with the psalmist:

O LORD, . . .
bring together all the peoples around you,
and rule over them from above. . . .
You are a righteous God
and judge our thoughts and desires. . . .
I thank the LORD for his justice;
I sing praises to the LORD, the Most High.
1, 7, 9, 17

What am I being asked to surrender to God?

Do not let evil defeat you;
instead, conquer evil with good. Romans 12:21

Write . . . everything
that I have told you."
Jeremiah 36:2

PRAYER JOURNAL–2

"Young Anne Frank began her journal
when her Jewish family went into hiding
in a warehouse in Amsterdam.
For two years they evaded the Nazis.
Finally they were discovered.
The police arrested them and
confiscated everything of apparent value.
They missed Anne's journal, however.
One entry read, "I can shake off everything
if I write. . . . My courage is reborn."

Anne's entry points to a second reason
for keeping a prayer journal. Its value
often lies not in the entries I write but
in what takes place inside me as I write.
Journaling is a proven way to help me
get in touch with my deeper, unknown self.
It tunes me in to the wordless conversation
going on in the sanctuary of my being
between God and myself.

This week I will continue and solidify
the practice of making a brief entry
in my journal after each meditation.
And I will continue
to address God in the first person.

When I gaze upon your sky,
O God, I am struck with awe.

A prisoner in a Nazi death camp
was standing next to a barbed-wire fence.
Suddenly the sun bloomed gold
against a clear blue sky. Then it happened.
A smile lit the prisoner's face.
His heart soared and he sang:
"The sun has made a veil of gold
So lovely that my body aches.
Above, the heavens shriek with blue—
Convinced I've smiled by some mistake.
The world's abloom and seems to smile.
I want to fly, but where, how high?
If in barbed wire things can bloom
Why cannot I? I will not die."   Author unknown
It was this kind of experience
that inspired the psalmist to write:

O LORD, . . . when I look at the sky,
which you have made, . . .
what are human beings,
that you think of them;
mere mortals, that you care for them?
You have made them inferior only to yourself;
you crowned them with glory.   1, 3–5

When did the world "bloom" and
wake within me new faith and new hope?

In the night of Death,
Hope sees a star, and listening Love
can hear the rustle of a wing.   Robert Ingersoll

Journal

25

Journal

O God, you do not turn away anyone who comes to you.

American prisoners of war in Vietnam
knew moments of fear and darkness.
Postwar interviews reveal that faith
played a big role in their ability to survive.
One prisoner said, "Without God
I would not have been able to survive."
The interviewer said to the soldier,
"In other words, God really helped you."
The prisoner replied, "No, not merely helped.
I mean it when I say I could not have made it
without God pulling me through."
Other prisoners
described worship services in the prisons,
composed of Bible readings put together
by the collective memory of the prisoners.

The LORD is a refuge for the oppressed,
a place of safety in times of trouble.
Those who know you, LORD, will trust you;
you do not abandon anyone
who comes to you. . . .
God remembers those who suffer;
he does not forget their cry. . . .
See the sufferings my enemies cause me!
Rescue me from death, O LORD.   9–10, 12–13

When was a time I put all my trust in God?

In the shadow of your wings
I find protection
until the raging storms are over.   Psalm 57:1

Why are you so far away, O God; why do you hide?

Journal

In her book *From Union Square to Rome*, Dorothy Day describes a time in jail when she was placed in solitary confinement: "Solitude and hunger and weariness of spirit—these sharpened my perceptions so that I suffered not only my own sorrows but the sorrows of those around me. . . . I was no longer a young girl, part of a radical movement seeking justice for those oppressed. I was the oppressed. . . . The only thoughts that brought comfort to my soul were those lines in the Psalms that expressed the terror and misery of one suddenly stricken and abandoned."

Why are you so far away, O LORD?
Why do you hide yourself . . . ?
The wicked are proud and persecute the poor;
catch them in the traps they have made. . . .
They spy on their helpless victims. . . .
The helpless victims lie crushed. . . .
O LORD, punish those wicked people!
1–2, 8, 10, 12

What keeps me from speaking out when I see blatant oppression taking place?

There are good men everywhere.
I only wish they had louder voices.
Louis L'Amour

Psalm 11 Day four

Journal

I trust in you, O God, even when all falls apart.

A prominent theme in the Psalms
is the confrontation between good and evil
that rages in our hearts and in our world.
Two strategies are open to us
when we confront evil face-to-face.
We can "fly away" and escape it,
or we can stand firm—and engage it.
Psalm 11 describes a person who chose
to stand firm and engage it, even though
a friend counseled him to "fly away."

I trust in the LORD for safety.
How foolish of you to say to me,
"Fly away like a bird to the mountains,
because . . . there is nothing a good person
can do when everything falls apart."
The LORD . . . watches people everywhere
and knows what they are doing. . . .
The LORD is righteous and loves good deeds;
those who do them will live in his presence.   1–4, 7

Somebody said, "There are three classes
of people: those who make things happen,
those who watch things happen,
those who have no idea what is happening.
Where would I locate myself—and why?

EVERYBODY was asked to do it.
EVERYBODY was sure SOMEBODY would do it.
ANYBODY could have done it.
But NOBODY did it.   Christopher News Notes

Keep us safe, O God, and preserve us.

In 1799 prophets of doom were predicting
that the end of the century
would also be the end of the world.
France had just endured a bloody revolution;
Europe was in chaos; the turmoil in Rome
was so bad that the cardinals had to meet
in Venice to elect a new pope.
Many believed this would be the last pope.
Psalm 12 took on prophetic meaning
for many people.

Honest people can no longer be found.
All of them lie to one another;
they deceive each other with flattery. . . .
O LORD! Close those boastful mouths that say,
"With our words we get what we want.
We will say what we wish, and no one
can stop us.". . . The wicked are everywhere,
and everyone praises what is evil.
Keep us always safe, O LORD,
and preserve us.   1–4, 7–8

In the year 4000 B.C.E. an Egyptian wrote,
"Our earth is degenerate. . . .
There are signs the world is ending."
What are my thoughts as I reflect
on the evil that is so prevalent in our world?

The confession of evil works
is the beginning of good works.
Saint Augustine

Journal

Journal

How long must I suffer, O God? Restore my strength.

Walter Ciszek, an American Jesuit,
spent twenty-three years in Russian prisons
and slave labor camps. He writes:
"One day . . . I was overwhelmed
by the hopelessness of my situation. . . .
I don't know how to put that moment
into words. . . . I knew that I had crossed over
the brink into a pit of blackness
I had never known before. . . .
I immediately turned to prayer
in fear and trembling."
What Father Ciszek experienced is almost
identical with what the psalmist experienced
in Psalm 13.

How much longer will you forget me, LORD?
Forever? How much longer
will you hide yourself from me?
How long must I endure trouble?
How long will sorrow fill my heart . . . ?
How long will my enemies triumph over me?
Look at me, O LORD my God, and answer me.
Restore my strength; don't let me die. 1–3

What situation in my life was similar
to that described by Father Ciszek
and the psalmist?

Hope is putting faith to work
when doubting would be easier.
E. C. McKenzie

O God, you behold a world in need of your salvation.

The Empire Strikes Back
is a kind of modern morality play.
The galaxy had fallen under the control
of the evil Darth Vader. Despair reigned.
No one gave young Luke Skywalker
much of a chance as he prepared
to do battle against the supertyrant.
But Luke knew something
that the rest of the galaxy did not know.
The Force was with him.
The world of evil into which Luke stepped
was akin to the world described in Psalm 14.

The LORD looks down from heaven . . .
to see if there are any who are wise,
any who worship him.
But they have all gone wrong;
they are all equally bad.
Not one of them does what is right,
not a single one.   2–3

Jesus stepped into this very world.
He too wasn't given much of a chance.
But he too knew what others did not know.
The Spirit was with him.
What can I do to open myself to the Spirit,
who wants to help me in my battle
against the forces of evil in our world?

None of us plans to fail.
We just fail to plan.   Author unknown

*"Go to your room,
close the door, and pray
to your Father, who is unseen."*
Matthew 6:6

PRAYER PLACE

*"Any place can be suitable for prayer. . . .
But if you want to pray undisturbed,
you would do well, if possible,
to find a special place in your home—
a consecrated place, so to speak—
and pray there."* Origen (second century)

A private place can be a great aid
to meditation. For example,
I might wish to pray lying down.
Or I might want to lift my arms heavenward.
Or I might wish to experiment
by speaking to God out loud. Of course,

I would hesitate to do these things in public.
And so my prayer would lack
a certain freedom and spontaneity.
The key thing about a prayer place
is that it helps me pray better.
Picking the right place is one of the keys
to effective meditation.

*This week I will try to settle on a place
for my meditation. If it doesn't work,
I will experiment with other places—
at my home, at my work, or on the bus.*

Who may enter your holy presence, O God?

Some students were talking about
how to succeed in the competitive world.
An older boy, obviously the leader, said,
"You've got to look out for yourself.
And if that means stepping on somebody,
then that's just too bad."
When a girl objected, the leader said,
"Look! It's a dog-eat-dog world. You gotta
make your own rules and play to win."
There comes a time when everyone
must decide whether to play by God's rules
or the world's rules.

LORD, who may enter your Temple?
Who may worship on Zion, your sacred hill?
Those who obey God in everything
and always do what is right,
whose words are true and sincere. . . .
They do no wrong to their friends
nor spread rumors about their neighbors. . . .
They always do what they promise,
no matter how much it may cost . . .
and cannot be bribed to testify
against the innocent.   1–5

How do I feel about playing by the rules?

This is the test. . . .
How much is there left in you
after you have lost everything
outside of yourself?   Author unknown

Journal

You have given me wonderful gifts, O God.

"I asked for health,
that I might do greater things;
I was given infirmity,
that I might do better things. . . .
I asked for riches, that I might be happy;
I was given poverty,
that I might be wise. . . .
I asked for power,
that I might have the praise of men;
I was given weakness,
that I might feel the need of God. . . .
I asked for all things,
that I might enjoy life;
I was given life,
that I might enjoy all things. . . .
I got nothing I asked for,
but everything I hoped for.
Almost despite myself,
my unspoken prayers were answered.
I am among all men most richly blessed."
Author unknown

"You, LORD, are all I have,
and you give me all I need. . . .
How wonderful are your gifts to me;
how good they are!" 5–6

Which of God's gifts to me do I value most?

God's gifts put man's best dreams to shame.
Elizabeth Barrett Browning

I have walked in your way, O God; save me.

An ancient Jewish story concerns a boy
who went to the synagogue every day.
His walk carried him past a fruit stand
owned by an atheist.
As the boy went by, the owner taunted him.
One day he told the boy, bluntly,
"You're wasting your time studying
about God. I'll give you this big red apple
if you can tell me where God is."
The boy thought a minute and said,
"Sir, I'll give you two big red apples
if you can tell me where God is not."
The faith that the boy manifested
is reflected in Psalm 17.

O LORD, . . . you know my heart. . . .
I have obeyed your command. . . .
I have always walked in your way
and have never strayed from it. . . .
Hide me in the shadow of your wings. . . .
Deadly enemies . . . are around me now,
wherever I turn, watching for a chance
to pull me down.   1, 3–5, 8–9, 11

What kind of witness am I in my world?

[Jesus said,] "You will stand
before rulers and kings . . .
to tell them the Good News. . . .
The words you speak will not be yours;
they will come from the Holy Spirit."
Mark 13:9, 11

Journal

O God, I called to you and you gave me victory.

In a dream a poet beheld
a cloud of dust on a great plain.
And in the cloud of dust a battle raged.
Brave soldiers shouted,
and swords clashed and snapped.
The king's banner fell to the ground,
trampled by foes.
A king's soldier thought,
"Had I the sword of the king's son—
rather than this half-broken thing!"
With that, he threw down his sword
and fled the cloud of dust.
The king's son, wounded and weaponless,
saw the broken sword and picked it up.
Crying out to heaven for help,
he plunged into the fray anew
and turned the tide of battle
that dark and wintry day.
Inspired by Edward Rolland Sill's "Opportunity"

The danger of death was around me,
and the grave set its trap for me. . . .
I called to my God for help. . . .
He rescued me from my powerful enemies. . . .
Praise my defender!
Proclaim the greatness of the God
who saves me.   5–6, 17, 46

With what trust do I call out to God?

Little love; little trust.   English proverb

How clearly the sky reveals your glory, O God.

Letters from the Desert is the journal
of Carlo Carretto, who went into the desert
to learn to pray. He writes:
"The first night spent here made me
send off for books on astronomy. . . .
I spent my free time learning a little
of what was passing over my head
up there in the universe. . . .
Kneeling on the sand I sank my eyes . . .
into those wonders. . . .
How dear they were to me, those stars;
how close to them the desert had brought me."
What Carlo saw, the psalmist saw too.
Filled with awe, he wrote:

How clearly the sky reveals God's glory!
How plainly it shows what he has done!
Each day announces it to the following day;
each night repeats it to the next.
No speech or words are used . . . ;
yet their message goes out to all the world
and is heard to the ends of the earth.   1–4

Jesus spent whole nights under the stars.
On those nights he probably recited Psalm 19.
What can I say to Jesus about those nights?

There's part of every star in every apple.
There's part of the moon in every rose.
There's part of God's flaming Pleiades
in every heart that prays.

Journal

Answer us, O God, when we call out to you.

Picture yourself in Jerusalem
the night before a great battle.
Beyond the city walls the enemy waits.
In the morning the king of Jerusalem
and his smaller army must defend the city.
Now the king sits on his throne.
Around him are his troops and subjects,
holding blazing torches.
The high priest stands, turns to the king,
and intones in a loud voice Psalm 20.

May the LORD answer you
when you are in trouble! . . .
May he send you help from his Temple. . . .
Then we will shout for joy
over your victory . . . by praising our God. . . .
Some trust in their war chariots
and others in their horses, but we trust
in the power of the LORD our God. . . .
Give victory to the king, O LORD;
answer us when we call. 1–2, 5, 7, 9

How deep is my faith and trust
that God is with me, strengthening and
supporting me in time of need?

Those who trust in the LORD for help
will find their strength renewed.
They will rise on wings like eagles;
they will run and not get weary . . .
walk and not grow weak. Isaiah 40:31

Your presence, O God, fills us with joy.

A fable describes a rooster who arrogantly believes the sun rises because he crows. Some people exhibit a similar arrogance. Israel's kings—at least the good ones— never had that problem.

They knew it was God who crowned them, defeated their foes, gave them wisdom, and blessed them beyond their wildest dreams. For these gifts, each good king was filled with joy and gratitude. The psalmist thanks God on the king's behalf.

The king is glad, O LORD,
because you gave him strength;
he rejoices
because you made him victorious.
You have given him his heart's desire;
you have answered his request.
You came to him with great blessings
and set a crown of gold on his head.
He asked for life,
and you gave it, a long and lasting life. . . .
Your blessings are with him forever,
and your presence fills him with joy.   1–4, 6

What are some blessings God has given me, and how am I using them for God's work?

Enter the Temple gates with thanksgiving;
go into its courts with praise.
Give thanks to him and praise him.   Psalm 100:4

39

Israel's Soul Book

David is traditionally given the credit
for authoring the Book of Psalms.
Actually, he probably wrote only a few.
Ancients commonly credited authorship
to a person who began or promoted
a literary undertaking.

The Book of Psalms has sometimes
been called Israel's Soul Book.
This is because it played an important role
in Israel's worship life.
It was both a *prayer book* and a *hymnbook*.

As Israel's *prayer book,*
it gives us a glimpse into Israel's soul.
We see how the people pray to God
in times of doubt, sorrow, and joy.

As Israel's *hymnbook,*
it gives us a glimpse into Israel's heart.
We see how the people celebrate,
especially in two settings.

The *first setting* is around a campfire.
A musician begins by strumming
a musical instrument; and the people—
especially the children—
join in, clapping, dancing, and singing.

*Listen [to the marvelous things] . . .
our ancestors told us.*

*We will not keep them from our children;
we will tell [them] . . .
about the LORD's power and
his great deeds.*   Psalm 78:1, 3–4

The *second setting* is the Temple,
especially on Jewish holy days.

Temple worship included
instrumental music, song, and dance.
It involved a chorus, dancers, musicians,
and the whole congregation.

Psalm 150 gives us an insight
into Temple worship.
The psalm takes only seconds to read
but took, perhaps, an hour to perform.

To catch its spirit, imagine a director
inviting each music group
to praise the Lord in its unique way.

*Praise [the LORD] with trumpets.
Praise [the LORD] with harps and lyres.
Praise [the LORD] with drums and dancing.
Praise [the LORD] with harps and flutes.
Praise [the LORD] with cymbals. . . .
Praise the LORD, all living creatures!*
Psalm 150:3–6

Journal

Early the next morning . . .
Jesus . . . went . . . to a lonely place,
where he prayed.   Mark 1:35

PRAYER TIME

The demands of modern living are such
that if we don't set aside a time each day
for meditating, we probably won't do it.
Some people don't like scheduling prayer.
"It's lacks spontaneity," they say.

———————

When something becomes important to me,
I don't leave it to chance.
I schedule it into my day.
Some "prayer times" I might consider are
• after showering in the morning,
• during the noon lunch break,
• just before supper,
• before retiring to bed.
Finding a time that fits my lifestyle
may take weeks of experimenting,
but it is worth the effort.
It is that important.

This week I will experiment
with a time for doing my meditation.
I might keep in mind that meditating
in the morning has the advantage
of praying while I am fresh
and tends to set the tone for my day.

My God, my God, why have you abandoned me?

Journal

An old Polish Jew who survived
the massacre of a Warsaw ghetto wrote:
"As I looked at that man upon the cross . . .
I knew I must make up my mind . . .
and either take my stand beside him and
share in his undefeated faith in God . . .
or else fall finally into a bottomless pit
of bitterness, hatred and unutterable despair."
S. Paul Shilling, *God in an Age of Atheism*
Jesus prayed Psalm 22 on the cross.

My God, my God,
why have you abandoned me?
I have cried desperately for help,
but still it does not come. . . .
My strength is gone,
gone like water spilled on the ground. . . .
My heart is like melted wax.
My throat is as dry as dust. . . .
My enemies look at me and stare.
They gamble for my clothes
and divide them among themselves. . . .
Come quickly to my rescue!   1, 14–15, 17–19

What are my thoughts as I look up at Jesus?

The crucified Jesus is a sign . . .
that love may suffer but it overcomes. . . .
The man of faith has found [in Jesus]
a hope stronger than history and a love
mightier than death.   Anthony Padovano

Journal

The Lord is my shepherd; I have everything I need.

"King Heroin is my shepherd;
I shall always want.
He maketh me lie down in gutters.
He leadeth me beside the troubled waters.
He destroyeth my soul.
He leadeth me in the paths of wickedness
for the effort's sake.
Yea, I shall walk through the valley of poverty
and will fear all evil, for thou,
Heroin, art with me.
Thy needle and capsule try to comfort me.
Thou strippest the table of groceries
in the presence of my family.
Thou robbest my head of reason.
My cup of sorrow runneth over.
Surely heroin addiction shall stalk me
all the days of my life, and I will dwell
in the House of the Damned forever."
Author unknown

The LORD is my shepherd;
I have everything I need. . . .
Even if I go through the deepest darkness,
I will not be afraid, LORD,
for you are with me.   1, 4

What is the nearest thing to an addiction
that I have?

Only the wearer knows
where the shoe pinches.   Proverb

Fling wide the gates; the great king will come in.

King David
ushered in Israel's "years of lightning."
He made Jerusalem not only Israel's
political center but also its religious center.
He ordered the building of a "sacred tent"
in which to place the Ark of the Covenant
(the sacred chest holding the two tablets
of the Ten Commandments).
When all was ready, the Ark was brought
to the city amid singing and dancing.
As the procession neared the ancient gates
of the walled city,
the people began singing Psalm 24.

Fling wide the gates, open the ancient doors,
and the great king will come in.
Who is this great king?
He is the LORD, strong and mighty,
the LORD, victorious in battle.
Fling wide the gates, open the ancient doors,
and the great king will come in.
Who is this great king?
The triumphant LORD . . . is the great king! 7–10

In my imagination I join the dancing, singing,
and waving of palms. What are my thoughts
as I march into the city?

Praise God . . . with drums and dancing. . . .
Praise the LORD, all living creatures!
Psalm 150:1, 4, 6

Journal

45

Journal

Teach me your ways, O God, and save me.

A poem describes a person
walking along a beach with the Lord.
Suddenly, happy and sad events
from the person's life flash across the sky.
Looking back at the footprints in the sand,
the person notices that during happy events
two sets of footprints appear on the sand.
During sad events only one set appears.
The person says to the Lord,
"I have noticed that during the most
troublesome times in my life,
there is only one set of footprints.
I don't understand why, in times
when I need you most, you would leave."
The Lord replies, "My precious child,
I would never leave you during
your times of trial and suffering.
When you see only one set of footprints,
it was then that I carried you."

Teach me your ways, O LORD;
make them known to me . . .
for you are my God, who saves me.   4–5

What can I say to Jesus about one time,
especially, that he carried me in my life?

"Do not be afraid or discouraged,
for I, the LORD your God,
am with you wherever you go."   Joshua 1:9

I love the house where you live, O God.

For Jews the Temple was the holiest place
on earth. Four courts led up to it:
court of the priests, court of the men,
court of the women, and court of the Gentiles.
People came to these courts daily to pray
and to present offerings for sacrifice
on an altar in front of the Temple.
Only priests were permitted
to approach the altar or to enter the Temple.
The holiest part of the Temple was the
Holy of Holies. Located behind a great curtain,
it concealed the Ark of the Covenant.
Inside the Ark were the stone tablets on
which were written the Ten Commandments.
Priests began each day by ritually purifying
themselves with water from a great bronze
basin. The psalmist describes the ritual:

LORD, I wash my hands . . .
and march in worship around your altar.
I sing a hymn of thanksgiving
and tell of all your wonderful deeds.
I love the house where you live, O LORD,
the place where your glory dwells.   6–8

How lovingly and joyfully do I worship
in the "house of my LORD"?

People study us Monday through Friday
to see what we mean
by our prayers and worship on Sunday.

Journal

Even if an army surrounds me, I will trust you, O God.

An amazing story came out of Armenia
concerning the 1989 earthquake
that killed thirty thousand people.
A father ran to his son's school building
and found it flattened.
Remembering the boy's classroom
was in the back right corner of the building,
he began digging, even though
everyone told him it was hopeless.
In the thirty-eighth hour of digging,
he heard his son's voice calling, "Dad!"
Incredibly, a tiny wedge shape had formed,
leaving just enough space for his son
and thirteen other boys to survive.
The son said to his dad, "I told the others
not to worry. I knew you'd come for me
and then they would be saved too."
The boy's trust in his dad
recalls the psalmist's trust in God.

The LORD protects me from all danger;
I will never be afraid. . . .
Even if a whole army surrounds me . . .
I will still trust God. . . .
In times of trouble he will shelter me;
he will keep me safe. 1, 3, 5

What gives some people so much trust?

In all things God works for good
with those who love him. Romans 8:28

Save your people, O God, and be our shepherd.

A woman had just learned she had cancer.
Suddenly her whole world collapsed.
She had never thought much about death.
Now she couldn't think of anything else.
She began to storm heaven for a miracle,
praying in the spirit of Psalm 28.

O LORD, my defender, I call to you.
Listen to my cry! If you do not answer me,
I will be among those who go down
to the world of the dead.
Hear me when I cry to you for help, when I
lift my hands toward your holy Temple. . . .
Save your people, LORD,
and bless those who are yours.
Be their shepherd,
and take care of them forever.   1–2, 9

What is my attitude toward cancer?

Cancer is so limited—
It cannot cripple love,
It cannot shatter hope,
It cannot corrode faith,
It cannot kill friendship,
It cannot suppress memories,
It cannot silence outrage,
It cannot invade the soul,
It cannot steal eternal life,
It cannot conquer the Spirit.
"What Cancer Cannot Do," *The Senior Times*

Journal

PRAYER POSTURE

Origen, a second-century Christian wrote:
"Of the many postures the body can assume
in prayer, the most preferable
is extending the hands and raising the eyes.
For the body is then showing the soul
how it should behave in prayer. . . .
But circumstances may be such that it is better
to pray sitting . . . even lying down."

How much would I give for a formula
that would make me look younger
and feel better? Probably a lot.
Yet the formula is built right into my body.

All I have to do is get into the habit
of checking my posture from time to time.
The truth is, posture has an amazing impact
on how I feel and think. This raises
the important question of prayer posture.
Once again, the best posture
is the one that helps me pray better.

This week I will experiment with different ways
of sitting—for example, back straight, feet flat
on the floor, hands resting with palms up
on the chair arms. If I feel venturesome,
I might try sitting cross-legged on the floor.

O God, your voice is heard in all its might and majesty.

"One night I was sleeping outside.
I was all alone because my camping partners
thought a thunderstorm was coming up.
They decided to sleep in a nearby shack.
Around midnight I awoke with a start.
The feeling of a storm filled the air.
Lightning was flashing everywhere.
Strangely enough, I wasn't at all afraid,
because God's presence seemed everywhere."
High school student (adapted)

An experience similar to the student's
may have inspired the writing of Psalm 29.
Called the "Song of the Seven Thunders,"
it mentions the voice of God seven times—
an allusion to the seven days of creation,
when God's voice called the world into being.

The voice of the LORD is heard on the seas;
the glorious God thunders. . . .
The voice of the LORD is heard
in all its might and majesty. . . .
The voice of the LORD
makes the lightning flash . . .
while everyone in his Temple shouts,
"Glory to God!" 3-4, 7, 9

When in my life did God seem to speak
to me through nature, especially a storm?

Earth is but a frozen echo
of the silent voice of God. Samuel Hageman

Journal

51

O God, you have changed my sadness into a joyful dance.

Some monks in Thailand
were moving a large clay statue of Buddha.
Their temple was being torn down
to make way for a modern freeway.
Suddenly the cart carrying the statue
hit a pothole, cracking the statue.
The monks were heartbroken.
Just then, however, they noticed
something shiny inside the crack.
It was a solid gold Buddha
concealed inside the clay statue.
Apparently, the gold statue had been coated
with clay centuries before to conceal it
from invading Burmese armies.
The two events that the monks thought
were catastrophes—losing their temple
and having the Buddha crack open—
turned out to be enormous blessings.
Psalm 30 celebrates a similar blessing.

*LORD, . . . you have changed my sadness
into a joyful dance; you have taken away
my sorrow and surrounded me with joy.
So I will not be silent; . . .
I will give you thanks forever.*   2, 11–12

When in my life did a cross
turn out to be an enormous blessing?

*Tears may flow in the night,
but joy comes in the morning.*   Psalm 30:5

I come to you, my God;
save me in your constant love.

Journal

Two soldiers named Tiira and Ericsson
grew disillusioned with the Foreign Legion.
One night they leaped from
the Legion's troop ship into the Indian Ocean.
For two weeks they drifted on a tiny raft
with no food to eat and only rain to drink.
Ericsson died on the seventeenth day.
Tiira continued to drift alone.
On the morning of the thirty-first day,
he knew death was near,
so he placed himself in God's hands.
Psalm 31 expresses the spirit of his prayer.
Shortly Tiira was found and rescued.
Jesus used Psalm 31 on the cross
to place himself in his Father's hands.

I come to you, LORD. . . .
I place myself in your care. . . .
Save me in your constant love.
I call to you, LORD;
don't let me be disgraced. . . .
How wonderful are the good things you keep
for those who honor you!   1, 5, 16–17, 19

When did I put myself completely
in God's hands? What might I say
to the crucified Jesus about it?

The LORD says . . . , "I can never forget you!
I have written your name
on the palms of my hands."   Isaiah 49:8, 16

Journal

I confessed my sins
and you forgave me, O God.

For two years, Paul Buchanan had avoided
the sacrament of Reconciliation.
He finally overcame his fear and went.
Then he celebrated by going for a drive.
He came upon a roadside chapel, stopped,
and went inside to look at it.
He wrote later: "Everything . . . had an air
of simple beauty. . . . Then, on the left side
of the sanctuary . . . I noticed a wooden lectern. . . .
On it was a Bible. . . .
I walked forward and began to read.
It was open to Psalm 32."

Happy are those whose sins are forgiven,
whose wrongs are pardoned. . . .
When I did not confess my sins,
I was worn out from crying all day long.
Day and night you punished me, LORD;
my strength was completely drained,
as moisture is dried up by the summer heat.
Then I confessed my sins to you;
I did not conceal my wrongdoings.
I decided to confess them to you,
and you forgave all my sins.   1, 3–5

How do I view "coincidences" like this?

Whoso draws nigh to God one step
through doubtings dim,
God will advance a mile
in blazing light to him.   Author unknown

By your word, O God, you created the universe.

"The earth is sacred!" Brave Buffalo
of Standing Rock came to this conclusion
early in life. He says:
"When I was ten years of age,
I looked at the land and the rivers,
the sky above and the animals around me,
and could not fail to realize
that they were made by some great power.
I was so anxious to understand this power
that I questioned the trees and the bushes."

The LORD created the heavens by his command,
the sun, moon, and stars by his spoken word.
He gathered all the seas into one place;
he shut up the ocean depths in storerooms.
Worship the LORD, all the earth!
Honor him, all peoples of the world!
When he spoke, the world was created;
at his command everything appeared. . . .
[The LORD's] plans endure forever;
his purposes last eternally. Happy is the nation
whose God is the LORD.   6–9, 11–12

What can I say to God about the sacredness
of creation and my loving respect for it?

I pledge my allegiance to the planet
and all the people on it;
to the soil and all the things beneath it;
to the sea and all that swims within it;
to the sky and all that soars across it.

O God, those who turn to you are never disappointed.

A Bible used by Lincoln in the White House
opens easily to Psalm 34.
A smudge in the margin of the page
shows where the president's thumb rested
as he meditated on it often.

I will always thank the LORD;
I will never stop praising him.
I will praise him for what he has done;
may all who are oppressed listen and be glad!
Proclaim with me the LORD's greatness;
let us praise his name together!
I prayed to the LORD, and he answered me;
he freed me from all my fears.
The oppressed look to him and are glad;
they will never be disappointed.
The helpless call to him, and he answers;
he saves them from all their troubles. . . .
Find out for yourself how good the LORD is.
Happy are those who find safety with him. . . .
The LORD is near to those
who are discouraged; he saves those
who have lost all hope.   1–6, 8, 18

Why do I think this psalm appealed to Lincoln?

Lord my God, give me
a mind to know you,
a heart to seek you,
wisdom to find you, and . . .
a hope of finally embracing you.   Thomas Aquinas

Journal

How much longer, O God, will you just look on?

Joel Filartiga serves as a medical doctor
to Paraguay's poorest of the poor.
He is also an outspoken protester
of Paraguay's oppressive political system.
To silence him, the police kidnapped
his teenage son and tortured him to death.
Instead of washing his son's body
and dressing it in clean clothes
to make it "presentable" to mourners,
Joel decided to do just the opposite.
He had his son laid out as he was found:
naked and wounded on a dirty, bloody mattress.
Psalm 35 gives us an insight into how
the teenaged victim must have felt.

*They were all glad
and gathered around to make fun of me;
strangers beat me and kept striking me.
Like those who would mock a cripple,
they glared at me with hate.
How much longer, Lord, will you just look on?
Rescue me from their attacks; save my life
from these lions! Then I will thank you
in the assembly of your people;
I will praise you before them all.*   15–18

What are my thoughts as I imagine myself
to be the son—or to be Joel as he looked
at his dead son?

Earth has no sorrow that heaven can't heal.
Thomas More

*Your presence
fills me with joy.*
Psalm 16:11

PRAYER AND PRESENCE–1

In John F. Kennedy: Man of the Sea, *Tazewell Taylor Shepard Jr. says Kennedy had on his desk a plaque from Admiral Rickover. It read: "O God, thy sea is so great, and my boat is so small."* Breton Fisherman's Prayer

---

This prayer focuses on the starting point
for all serious meditation.
It is standing consciously in God's presence.
This means I try to focus on God's greatness.
I try to zero in on the incredible fact
that this "great God" is more present
to me than I am to myself.

An experience—or "sensible awareness"
of God's presence—is a tremendous gift.
Occasionally God will give it to me.
When this happens, I simply rest in God's
presence as long as God gives it to me.
Any effort to try to "feel" God's presence
is usually always wrong. I cannot wish it
or will it. It is simply a "gift" from God.

*This week I will make a special effort
to open myself to an awareness
of God's presence as I begin my meditation.*

Your love and fidelity, O God, reach to the heavens.

In his play *Long Day's Journey into Night*, Eugene O'Neill has Edmund describe a mystical experience. Actually, it was one that O'Neill himself had one night on a square-rigger bound for Buenos Aires: "For a moment, I lost myself. . . . I became the white sails and flying spray, became the beauty and the rhythm, became the moonlight and the ship and the dim-starred sky! I belonged . . . within something greater than my own life . . . To God if you want . . . and several other times in my life, when I was swimming far out, or lying alone on the beach, I have had the same experience." The psalmist responds to such an experience when he says to God ecstatically:

Your constant love reaches the heavens;
your faithfulness extends to the skies. . . .
Your justice is like the depths of the sea. . . .
How precious, O God, is your constant love! . . .
You are the source of all life, and
because of your light we see the light.   5–7, 9

Can I recall an experience like O'Neill's?

[I] was snatched up to the highest heaven . . .
(I do not know whether this actually happened
or whether it was a vision—only God knows),
and . . . heard things which cannot be put
into words.   2 Corinthians 12:2–4

Journal

Worry and anger, O God, lead only to trouble.

Ralph Waldo Emerson had just ended a lecture. The emcee asked a minister to conclude with a prayer. The minister prayed, "Lord, deliver us from ever having to hear any more of such . . . nonsense." When asked about the minister's prayer, Emerson said, "He was quite outspoken." Emerson's response to the minister's attack followed the advice of Psalm 37.

Seek your happiness in the LORD. . . .
Don't give in to worry or anger;
it only leads to trouble.   4, 8

How do I respond to people who attack or ridicule me because they disagree with me?

People are unreasonable,
illogical and self-centered.
Love them anyway! . . .
The biggest man with the biggest ideas
can be shot down
by the smallest men with the smallest minds.
Think big anyway! . . .
What you spend years building
may be destroyed overnight.
Build anyway! . . .
Give the world the best you have
and you'll get kicked in the teeth.
Give the world the best you've got anyway!
Theodore Roethke

My heart is troubled.
Help me, O God.

"[It is Sunday afternoon in Zunil, a poor town
in Guatemala. I set off] to anoint and pray for
a young girl who is very sick. I am met
at the door by her father and ushered
into a dark one-room dirt-floor adobe. . . .
For months now she has been lying
on this mat on the dirt floor. . . .
I speak to her in halting Spanish.
Her sorrowful brown eyes follow
my every move. I give her the sacrament
of the Anointing of the Sick. . . .
Finally I bless this lovely girl whose life
is so cruelly cut off by what is so easily
avoidable: the shoes she didn't have . . .
the medicine that wasn't given her."
John Eagan, *A Traveller Toward the Dawn*

I am burning with fever and I am near death.
I am worn out and utterly crushed;
my heart is troubled, and I groan with pain. . . .
My friends and
neighbors will not come near me. . . .
But I trust in you, O LORD. . . .
Do not abandon me. . . .
Help me now, O Lord my savior!   7–8, 11, 15, 21–22

What do I say to Jesus about the plight
of the afflicted—especially the young?

There is more evil in a drop of sin
than in a sea of affliction.   Thomas Watson

Journal

How short you have made my life, O God!

Gertrude Ederle dove into the French sea.
Her destination was England.
Fourteen hours and thirty-one minutes later,
she emerged from the water.
She had just swum the English Channel faster
than any human being had ever done.
Europe fell at her feet. New York went wild.
Years later she observed,
"When they gave a parade for me,
others who had been there before my time
watched it. Now I'm watching parades."
Gertrude Ederle saw the fleeting nature
of fame much as the psalmist saw
the fleeting nature of life.

How short you have made my life!
In your sight my lifetime seems nothing.
Indeed every living being is no more
than a puff of wind, no more than a shadow.
All we do is for nothing; we gather wealth,
but don't know who will get it.
What, then, can I hope for, Lord? 5–7

Can I recall an "hour of glory" in my life?
What really counts in life for me?

"[A man was rejoicing in his acquisition
of wealth.] God said to him, 'You fool!
This very night you will have to give up
your life; then who will get all these things
you have kept for yourself?'" Luke 12:20

Tragedy overtakes me, O God.

Herb Score was the toast of Cleveland.
The 23-year-old had won twenty games
and led both leagues in strikeouts.
Then came the night of May 7, 1958.
Pitching against the Yankees,
Herb had a 2–2 count on Gil McDougald.
Gil hit the next pitch like a bullet—
into Herb's face. Herb fell to the ground,
blood pouring from his right eye.
He said later, "I was afraid I was blind,
and I prayed to God."
Herb's sight returned,
but in spite of prayer and strenuous effort,
his pitching form never did.
Herb rejoiced in what had been,
and set out on a new life as a sportscaster.

[The LORD]
pulled me out of a dangerous pit. . . .
He set me safely on a rock
and made me secure.
He taught me to sing a new song,
a song of praise to our God. . . .
You have given me ears to hear you. . . .
"How I love to do your will, my God!
I keep your teaching in my heart." 2–3, 6, 8

When have I experienced a spirit like Herb's?

The test of whether our heart is right
is that we will what God wills. Anonymous

Journal

Journal

O God, happy are they who help the poor.

Former Governor Pat Brown of California
spent three weeks working in Calcutta
at Mother Teresa's home for dying
street people. He writes:
"It was not unusual to have to clean up
a patient after he soiled himself.
After doing it a couple of times,
it became fairly easy. I kept reminding myself
of Mother Teresa's words. . . .
'What you do for him, [you do for Christ].' . . .
That is what got to me: the dignity
given people who had absolutely nothing.
What a world it would be if somehow
this became the predominant spirit."
Life magazine (April 1988)

*Happy are those
who are concerned for the poor;
the Lord will help them
when they are in trouble. . . .
The Lord will help them when they are sick
and will restore them to health. . . .
My enemies say cruel things about me.
They want me to die. . . .
They say, "He is fatally ill;
he will never leave his bed again."*   1, 3, 5, 8

Why would/wouldn't I do what Brown did?

"I was sick and you took care of me."
Matthew 25:36

As a deer longs for water, O God, so I thirst for you.

Screenwriter Dan Wakefield returned
to church after years of absence, saying:
"The practice of regular attendance
at Sunday service, which such a short time
ago seemed religiously 'excessive,'
no longer seemed enough.
Whatever it was I was getting from church
on Sunday morning,
I wanted—needed . . . more of it.
I experienced what is a common phenomenon
for people who . . . begin a journey of this
kind . . . a feeling . . . best described as
a 'thirst . . . for God.' " *Returning: A Spiritual Journey*

As a deer longs
for a stream of cool water,
so I long for you, O God.
I thirst for you, the living God. . . .
Here in exile my heart is breaking,
and so I turn my thoughts to him. . . .
I will put my hope in God,
and once again I will praise him,
my savior and my God. 1–2, 6, 11

To what extent do I find myself trying
to assuage a spiritual thirst or hunger
with a physical substitute?

To exist is to change, to change is
to mature, to mature is to go on
creating oneself endlessly. Henri Bergson

III

Themes of the Psalms

The movie *The Sound of Music* contains a show-stopping song called "Maria." One line from the song asks, "How can you hold a moonbeam in your hand?" That line celebrates the fact that Maria is so special that she is in a class by herself.

Many of the psalms are like Maria. Trying to classify them is like trying to hold a moonbeam in our hand. A traditional classification arranges them in five groups: praise, wisdom, royal, thanksgiving, and lament.

Praise psalms concern God's glory and often begin with the words "Praise God." "Praise God in his Temple! . . . Praise the LORD, all living creatures!" (Psalm 150:1, 6).

Wisdom psalms concern human conduct and often begin with the words "Happy are those" (Psalm 41:1).

Royal psalms concern the king. Starting with God's promise to David, the king became more than a political figure. He became a religious symbol as well.

Each new king brought Israel closer to the "King of Kings," the promised Messiah. And so psalms were composed to celebrate this fact. Take Psalm 101. It sounds like the king's oath of office:

I will live a pure life in my house
and will never tolerate evil. . . .
I will destroy the wicked in our land.   2–3, 8

Thanksgiving psalms express gratitude to God for benefits and blessings:

You have changed my sadness
into a joyful dance;
you have taken away my sorrow
and surrounded me with joy. . . .
LORD, you are my God;
I will give you thanks forever.   Psalm 30:11–12

Finally, lament psalms are "songs of woe" in which the psalmist pours out his heart to God about some situation. These psalms often deal with defeat or injury at the hand of an enemy.

I lie awake;
I am like a lonely bird on a housetop.
All day long my enemies insult me.   Psalm 102:7–8

Whether or not we can fit the psalms into neat categories is unimportant. What is important is whether or not they speak to the heart.

Journal

The LORD . . .
lets me rest . . . and leads me
to quiet pools of fresh water. Psalm 23:1–2

PRAYER AND PRESENCE–2

The starting point for serious meditation
is opening oneself
to an awareness of God's presence.
One way to do this is to create an atmosphere
of quiet and calm. A procedure for doing this
is to relax the body completely.
The procedure is simple.

My body has three major tension zones.
The first is the forehead.
Under stress I wrinkle it.
This only makes things worse.
I relax it and my problems seem smaller.

The second tension zone is the jaw.
Under stress I tend to clench it, sending
a message to my brain: "I've got a problem!"
I relax the jaw and the warning is canceled.
The third zone is the chest. Under stress
it tends to tighten, restricting breathing.
When the stress subsides, I sigh, "Now that
I have that off my chest I can breathe again."

This week I will open myself to an awareness
of God's presence by relaxing the tension zones
of the body before beginning
the opening prayer for my meditation.

O God, declare me innocent, and defend my cause.

Dead Man Walking is a book by Helen Prejean. She lists a number of relatively recent cases of people sent to death row and later found to be innocent. One was Anthony Brown, a Florida man sentenced to die in 1983. Errors in his first trial resulted in a new trial in which the prosecution's chief witness admitted lying under oath.

A second innocent man was Randall Adams. The Texas Court of Criminal Appeals set aside his murder conviction in 1989 when it was proven that prosecutors created evidence and used the perjured testimony of the actual murderer.

Both innocent men could relate to Psalm 43, in which the psalmist cries out in anguish:

O God, declare me innocent,
and defend my cause against the ungodly;
deliver me from lying and evil people!
You are my protector. . . . Why must I go on
suffering from the cruelty of my enemies?
Send your light and your truth. . . .
I will put my hope in God,
and once again I will praise him,
my savior and my God.   1–3, 5

When could I have prayed these words?

I don't think of the misery but of the beauty that still remains.   Anne Frank

Journal

O God, you have let us be defeated. Come to our aid.

Picture thousands of villagers and farmers
running through the great gates of the walls
that encircle and protect Jerusalem.
The Judean army has been routed in battle,
and all are in a state of fear and panic.
They stream into the Temple court,
fall on their knees, and cry out to God:

With our own ears we have heard . . .
how you yourself drove out the heathen
and established your people in their land;
how you punished the other nations
and caused your own to prosper. . . .
But now you have rejected us
and let us be defeated. . . .
You made us run from our enemies. . . .
You allowed us to be slaughtered. . . .
Our neighbors see what you did to us. . . .
You have made us a joke among the nations. . . .
We fall crushed to the ground;
we lie defeated in the dust. Come to our aid!
Because of your constant love save us!
1–2, 9–11, 13–14, 25–26

How does my personal life—
at times, perhaps—parallel the collective life
of the people of Judah?

Courage is not the absence of fear
but the ability to carry on with dignity
in spite of it.   Scott Turow

O God, beautiful words fill my mind.

Jerusalem was aglow with excitement.
It was the day of the royal wedding.
For months, anticipation had been mounting.
And at last the long-awaited day had come.
The king and the queen looked upon their vows
as a sacred covenant
not unlike the one between God and Israel.
Psalm 45 alternates
addressing the king and the queen.

Beautiful words fill my mind,
as I compose this song for the king. . . .
The kingdom that God has given you
will last forever and ever. . . .
You love what is right and hate what is evil.
That is why God, your God, has chosen you. . . .
Bride of the king, listen to what I say—
forget your people and your relatives.
Your beauty will make the king desire you. . . .
You, my king, will have many sons
to succeed your ancestors as kings,
and you will make them rulers
over the whole earth. 1, 6–7, 10–11, 16

"When a marriage works, nothing on earth
can take its place." Helen Gahagan Douglas
What is one key to making a marriage work?

Two people who love each other
are in a place more holy
than the interior of a church. William Lyon Phelps

Journal

O God, we will not fear, even if the earth be shaken.

TV photographer David Crocket of KOMO-TV, Seattle, was caught at the foot of Mount Saint Helens when it erupted on the morning of May 18, 1980. For ten hours he was trapped and nearly buried alive by millions of tons of volcanic ash and debris. Miraculously, a helicopter spotted and saved him. "During those ten hours," David said, "I saw a mountain fall apart. I saw a forest disappear. I saw that God is the only one who is unmovable. I feel somehow that I'm being allowed to start over . . . whatever is in his master plan for me." Today on David's wall is a photograph of Mount Saint Helens. In the corner of it are these words of Psalm 46:

God is our shelter . . . ,
always ready to help in times of trouble.
So we will not be afraid,
even if the earth is shaken
and mountains fall. . . .
The LORD Almighty is with us;
the God of Jacob is our refuge.   1–2, 7

Have I ever felt that God was giving me a chance "to start over"? Do I believe God has a master plan for me?

Life is fragile—handle with prayer.
E. C. McKenzie

You are king, O God, over all the earth.

Each year Israel recrowned its king
in a kind of anniversary celebration.
It seems that the great event began
with a reenactment of the history of salvation:
God's promise to Abraham,
God's covenant with Israel at Mount Sinai,
God's messianic promise to David.
Following the reenactment,
the king was recrowned.
The celebration ended with a look
into the future, when God would mount
God's throne in heaven and fulfill the promise
to bless all nations through Israel (Genesis 12:2).

Clap your hands for joy, all peoples!
Praise God with loud songs! . . .
He gave us victory over the peoples;
he made us rule over the nations.
He chose for us the land where we live,
the proud possession of his people,
whom he loves. God goes up to his throne.
There are shouts of joy
and the blast of trumpets,
as the LORD goes up.
Sing praise to God; sing praise to our king!
God is king over all the world.   1, 3–7

How does this psalm speak ultimately of Jesus
and his eternal kingship?

Come, Lord Jesus!   Revelation 22:20

Journal

Your city, O God, brings joy to the world.

Ancients believed a great mountain existed
in the "far recesses of the North."
It soared skyward, piercing heaven itself.
Atop the mountain lived the gods.
Israel borrowed this image and applied it
to the mount on which the walled city
of Jerusalem was built.
The city's highest point was called Zion.
Upon it the Temple was built.

The LORD is great and is to be highly praised
in the city of our God, on his sacred hill.
Zion, the mountain of God,
is high and beautiful;
the city of the great king brings joy
to all the world. . . .
We have heard what God has done, and now
we have seen it in the city of our God. . . .
Inside your Temple, O God,
we think of your constant love.
You are praised by people everywhere, and
your fame extends over all the earth.   1–2, 8–10

What I can do to make the divine fame
extend not only where I live
but "over all the earth"?

Who has the right to go up the LORD's hill?
Who may enter his holy Temple?
Those who are pure in act and in thought.
Psalm 24:3–4

O God, you will rescue me and save me.

Thornton Wilder's novel *The Eighth Day*
is about a family whose days on earth
are filled with misfortune and oppression.
Yet the family never grows bitter
nor loses faith in God.
The novel ends
without the good family being rewarded
or the evil villains being punishment.
Wilder suggests, however,
that the family's plight is like a tapestry.
From one viewpoint (the world's) it is ugly.
From another viewpoint (God's) it is glorious.
The psalmist suggests something similar.

Hear this, everyone!
Listen, all people everywhere,
great and small alike, rich and poor. . . .
Our greatness cannot keep us from death. . . .
See what happens to those
who trust in themselves, . . .
who are satisfied with their wealth—
they are doomed to die like sheep,
and Death will be their shepherd. . . .
But God will rescue me; he will save me.
1–2, 12–15

How do I feel about the fate of each group?

What we suffer at this present time
cannot be compared at all with the glory
that is going to be revealed to us.   Romans 8:18

Journal

PRAYER AND PRESENCE–3

The starting point for serious meditation
is opening oneself to an awareness
of God's presence.
We saw that one way to do this
is to create an atmosphere of quiet and calm.
Another way is to monitor one's breathing.
The procedure is simple.

———————

I close my eyes, relax my body,
and count out ten exhalations.
Then I open my eyes and say this prayer
slowly and from the heart:

"My God.
you are closer to me than my own breath.
May each breath I take
deepen my awareness of your presence
in the temple of my body."

Then, when I am ready,
I begin my meditation,
following the "Daily Meditation Format"
on the front end sheet of this book.

This week, to create an atmosphere of quiet
and calm, I will begin each meditation
by monitoring my breathing.

O God, I called to you
in my trouble and you saved me.

Journal

Mel Bitters and his wife
were sailing on a lake in Maine.
Suddenly a storm blew up,
capsizing their boat and blowing it away.
Despite their efforts to stay together,
they became separated.
They drifted farther and farther apart.
Mel kept shouting through the storm
to his wife, but got no response.
His heart sank as he thought of the agony
of telling his six children, "Mother is dead."
Then, out of nowhere, two lines
from Psalm 50 flashed across his mind:
"Call to me when trouble comes;
I will save you, and you will praise me."
Mel called with all his might.
Minutes later, both he and his wife
were spotted and saved by a search craft.

[The LORD says,] "I am God, your God. . . .
Call to me when trouble comes;
I will save you, and you will praise me." . . .
"Giving thanks is the sacrifice that honors me,
and I will surely save all who obey me." 7, 15, 23

What can I recall about a time when I called
to God in time of trouble and God saved me?

More things are wrought by prayer
Than this world dreams of. Alfred Lord Tennyson

Journal

O God, create in me a new heart and a new spirit.

Thomas Merton had just graduated from
high school and was traveling alone in Europe.
His father and his mother were both dead,
and he was living a wayward life.
One night, in the silence of his room,
he underwent a soul-stirring experience.
He writes in *The Seven Storey Mountain:*
"I was overwhelmed with a sudden
and profound insight into the misery
and corruption of my own soul. . . .
I was filled with horror at what I saw. . . .
And now I think for the first time in my life
I really began to pray . . . , praying to the God
I had never known to reach down . . . and help me
to get free of the thousand terrible things
that held my will in their slavery."

O God, . . . make me clean from my sin! . . .
Create a pure heart in me, O God,
and put a new and loyal spirit in me. . . .
Give me again the joy that comes
from your salvation.   1–2, 10, 12

How can I ask Jesus for the grace to see myself
with the honesty and clarity
that Merton described, and for the courage
to do whatever the Spirit seems to suggest?

Repentance is not self-regarding,
but God-regarding. It is not self-loathing,
but God-loving.   Fulton J. Sheen

O God, those who love evil are doomed to be ruined.

Some boys were conversing loudly on a train.
One boy boasted that he cheated all the time
and found it easy and profitable.
After listening to the boaster for a while,
a mild-looking man across the aisle leaned over
and said to the boy, "All the same—
I'd keep one eye on the law of the echo."
Arthur Gordon, who tells the story, asks,
"Is there such a thing as the 'law of the echo,'
namely, that whatever you send out—
honesty or dishonesty, kindness or cruelty—
will ultimately return to you in kind?"
The psalmist does not answer the question
directly, but he warns people, like the boy,
about something even more disturbing.

Why do you boast, great one, of your evil? . . .
You love evil more than good
and falsehood more than truth. . . .
So God will ruin you. . . .
Righteous people will . . . laugh at you
and say, "Look, here is someone
who did not depend on God . . .
[but] looked for security in being wicked." 1, 3, 5–7

Do I feel there is such a thing
as the law of the echo—
that what I send out has a way of returning?

You will reap
exactly what you plant. Galatians 6:7

Journal

O God, you behold a world in need of salvation.

Years ago a popular sitcom on television
was *The Mary Tyler Moore Show.*
In one of the show's episodes,
Mary gets fed up with the world
and says to her journalist boss, Mr. Grant,
"It's a lousy business we're in, Mr. Grant;
I quit. I'm going to Africa
to work with Albert Schweitzer."
Mr. Grant looks at her amazed and says,
"Mary, Albert Schweitzer is dead!"
Without blinking an eye, Mary says,
"You see what I mean, Mr. Grant?
It's a lousy world."
There were times when the psalmist
felt the same way.

God looks down from heaven at people
to see if there are any who are wise,
any who worship him.
But . . . they are all equally bad.
Not one of them does what is right,
not a single one. . . .
"They live by robbing my people,
and they never pray to me." 2–4

If I were asked to make one suggestion for
reforming our world, what would I suggest?

Reformers waste their time trying
to clean up horse races; it's the human race
that needs cleaning up. E. C. McKenzie

You have rescued me, O God, from all my troubles.

In October 1945 Branch Rickey signed
Jackie Robinson as the first black athlete
in the big leagues. Before the contract
was inked, Rickey told Jackie,
"You will have to take everything they dish out
and never strike back." Rickey was right.
Through it all Jackie kept his cool.
In 1947 he was named Rookie of the Year.
In 1949 he won the league batting title.
In 1961 he was elected to the Hall of Fame.
In the midst of his struggle,
Jackie was certainly reminded
of these words of Psalm 54:

Save me by your power, O God. . . .
Proud people are coming to attack me;
cruel people are trying to kill me—
those who do not care about God. . . .
I will gladly offer you a sacrifice, O LORD;
I will give you thanks. . . .
You have rescued me from all my troubles,
and I have seen my enemies defeated.   1, 3, 6–7

How does the story of Jackie Robinson
speak to me?

Don't be blinded by prejudice,
disheartened by the times. . . .
Don't let anything paralyze your mind,
tie your hands, or defeat your spirit.
Walter Fauntroy

Journal

O God, a former friend has turned against me.

George Washington was extremely sensitive, especially to criticism.
In a letter to his wife, Martha, he wrote:
"You can imagine my feelings as I reread Thomas Paine's last letter to me.
He and I were once friends. As his friend, I tried to get the Virginia legislature to vote him a pension or grant of land.
And yet, because I did not think him qualified to become postmaster general, he charged me with being treacherous in a private friendship."

If it were an enemy . . . ,
I could endure it;
if it were an opponent . . . ,
I could hide myself from him.
But it is you, my companion,
my colleague and close friend.
We had intimate talks with each other
and worshiped together in the Temple. . . .
My former companion attacked his friends. . . .
His words . . . cut like sharp swords.   12–14, 20–21

How do I respond when someone I respect seems to turn on me? How would/did Jesus respond to such a situation?

Son, never do a wrong thing
to make a friend or to keep one.
    Robert E. Lee to his son at West Point

You rescued me, O God, and kept me from defeat.

In his last speech before he was shot,
Martin Luther King Jr.
seemed to have a premonition of death.
Speaking of his funeral, he said:
"If you get somebody to deliver the eulogy,
tell him not to talk too long.
Tell him not to mention
that I have three or four hundred awards.
That's not important. Tell them . . .
that Martin Luther King Jr. tried to love. . . .
I want you to say on that day
that I tried to love and serve humanity."
In his final days, these words of the psalmist
spoke deeply to Dr. King:

Be merciful to me, O God,
because I am under attack;
my enemies persecute me all the time.
All day long my opponents attack me. . . .
I trust in God and am not afraid;
I praise him for what he has promised.
What can a mere human being do to me? . . .
And so I walk in the presence of God,
in the light that shines on the living.   1–2, 4, 13

What keeps me from trusting God as I should?

God is our shelter and strength. . . .
So we will not be afraid, even if
the earth is shaken and the mountains
fall into the ocean depths.   Psalm 46:1–2

Journal

83

PRAYER AND PRESENCE–4

The starting point for serious meditation
is opening oneself to an awareness
of God's presence.
One way to do this is to create an atmosphere
of quiet and calm by monitoring one's breathing.
Another way
is to listen to the sounds around oneself.
The procedure is simple.

———

I close my eyes, relax my body,
and listen to the sounds around me
for about twenty seconds.
Then I open my eyes and say this prayer
slowly and from the heart:

"My God,
you are more real than the sounds around me.
May each sound I hear
deepen my awareness of your presence."

Then, when I am ready,
I begin my meditation,
following the "Daily Meditation Format"
on the front end sheet of this book.

This week, to create an atmosphere of quiet
and calm, I will begin each meditation
by listening to the sounds around me.

In you, O God,
I have complete confidence.

As David's military fame soared,
Saul was seized with fits of jealousy.
During one of these fits, David fled
to an area where there were many caves.
Saul learned of his whereabouts, gathered
a huge posse, and pursued him (1 Samuel 24:2).
One day Saul stopped to rest in the very cave
where David was hiding.
Ancient Jews saw Psalm 57 as a reflection
of David's state of mind at that time.

I am surrounded by enemies,
who . . . have spread a net to catch me. . . .
[But] I have complete confidence,
O God; I will sing and praise you! . . .
I will thank you, O Lord. . . .
Your constant love reaches the heavens;
your faithfulness touches the skies.
Show your greatness in the sky, O God,
and your glory over all the earth.   4, 6–7, 9–11

The stained-glass window of the Prayer Room
in the U.S. Capitol reads, "Preserve me, O God;
for in thee do I put my trust" (Psalm 16:1).
What keeps me from praying this verse
as trustfully as I would like?

Though the path be dark at night,
There's a star to guide the humble;
Trust in God and do the right.
          Norman Macleod

Journal

O God, you will pass judgment on evildoers.

A young policeman
was attacked while writing a traffic ticket
in an area of Dallas that was hostile to police.
Someone grabbed
the officer's gun from its holster
while one or two people cheered
and goaded him into shooting the officer.
He did! Three times in the face!
Some in the crowd
advised the gunman to flee.
No one helped the downed officer.
Psalm 58 reflects the outrage
many citizens felt toward the assailant
and the crowd.
We may not relate to the psalm's imagery,
but we can to its outrage.

Break the teeth of these fierce lions, O God.
May they disappear like water draining away;
may they be crushed like weeds on a path. . . .
The righteous will be glad
when they see sinners punished. . . .
People will say, ". . . there is indeed a God
who judges the world."   6–7, 10–11

How do I respond to the evil in our world?

The only thing necessary
for the triumph of evil
is for good people to do nothing.
Edmund Burke (slightly adapted)

O God, you are my refuge; save me.

As David's military fame soared,
Saul was seized with uncontrollable fits of envy.
One day as Saul sat with a spear in his hand,
David was calmly playing his harp nearby.
Suddenly Saul hurled the spear at David.
David dodged, the spear stuck in the wall,
and David fled. "That same night
Saul sent some men to watch David's house
and kill him the next morning" (1 Samuel 19:11).
Ancient Jews saw Psalm 59
as a reflection of David's state of mind
when he saw henchmen surround his house.

Save me from my enemies, my God. . . .
Look! They are waiting to kill me;
cruel people are gathering against me.
It is not because of any sin or wrong . . .
that they hurry to their places. . . .
But I will sing about your strength; . . .
I will sing aloud of your constant love. . . .
My refuge is God, the God who loves me. 1, 3–4, 16–17

What are my thoughts as I imagine myself
to be David?

Henry Van Dyke proposes four goals that,
like young David, we must seek to cultivate:
To think without confusion clearly;
To love his fellow-men sincerely;
To act from honest motives purely;
To trust in God and heaven securely.

Journal

O God, with you on our side, we cannot lose.

Nazi oppression of Jews escalated.
Fear was everywhere. A young Jew wrote:
"One afternoon I looked out the window
and saw some sparrows hopping around. . . .
For a fleeting moment, I envied those birds.
How carefree they were!
How easily they could fly across borders. . . .
A question came to my mind:
'Does God take care of the sparrows? . . .
And if he takes care of them—
perhaps he will help me, too.'
For the first time I felt a glimmer of hope,
and my heart felt a little lighter."
Paul Waldemann, *Richer Than a Millionaire*

You have rejected us, God. . . .
You have made your people suffer greatly;
we stagger around. . . .
Save us by your might; answer our prayer,
so that the people you love may be rescued. . . .
Help us against the enemy;
human help is worthless.
With God on our side we will win;
he will defeat our enemies.   1, 3, 5, 11–12

What gives me hope when skies darken?

Let us be like a bird for a moment perched
On a frail branch while he sings;
Though he feels it bend, yet he sings his song,
Knowing that he has wings.   Victor Hugo

O God, you are my protector, my strong defense.

A woman was seated at a window, reading.
She looked up from her book
and saw a fly crawling across the glass.
Suddenly a lizard appeared
on the other side of the windowpane.
It saw the fly and stretched out its tongue
to snatch it.
To the woman's surprise, the fly kept crawling,
totally undisturbed by the lizard's presence.
Somehow it sensed
that it was protected by the windowpane.
"That windowpane,"
said the woman, "is an image of God.
God is always there
to guard and protect us from spiritual evil."
The psalmist alludes
to God's protective presence in Psalm 61.

You are my protector,
my strong defense against my enemies.
Let me live in your sanctuary all my life;
let me find safety under your wings. . . .
I will always sing praises to you.   3–4, 8

How might I become more aware
of God's protective presence in my life?

Behind the dim unknown,
Standeth God within the shadow,
Keeping watch above his own.
        James Russell Lowell

Journal

Journal

O God, I wait patiently for you to save me.

It began as a four-day hike up Mount Hood.
About 9,000 feet up, a blinding blizzard hit.
Teenager Gary Schneider and two friends
dug a snow cave to wait out the storm.
Their greatest comfort was a small Bible,
which one of the boys had in his backpack.
The Book of Psalms, especially,
gave them support, particularly Psalm 62.

I wait patiently for God to save me. . . .
I depend on God alone. . . .
My salvation and honor depend on God;
he is my strong protector;
he is my shelter.
Trust in God at all times, my people.
Tell him all your troubles,
for he is our refuge.   1, 5, 7–8

Sixteen days later, with a few spoonfuls
of pancake batter left, the weather cleared
and the boys were rescued.
Can I recall a time when I had to put
all my trust in God? Do I have an ability
to trust, just as the three boys did?

Have courage
for the great sorrows of life
and have patience for the small ones;
and when you have
laboriously achieved your daily task,
go to sleep in peace. God is awake.   Victor Hugo

I cling to you, O God;
your hand keeps me safe.

General ("Old Blood and Guts") Patton died
just before Christmas in 1945. What the might
of the German army could not do to him,
a car accident did. The *New York Times* wrote,
"Patton was a legend. Spectacular, swaggering,
pistol-packing, deeply religious and
violently profane, easily moved to tears
because . . . he had a kind heart,
he was a strange combination of fire and ice."
Describing his burial,
his biographer Ladislas Farago wrote,
"Patton was sent on his long journey
with the Psalm David had sung in the wilderness
of Judah . . . Patton's own favorite [Psalm 63]."

O God, you are my God, and I long for you.
My whole being desires you. . . .
I will give you thanks as long as I live;
I will raise my hands to you in prayer. . . .
I will sing glad songs of praise to you. . . .
In the shadow of your wings I sing for joy.
I cling to you, and your hand keeps me safe.
1, 4–5, 7–8

How honestly can I pray
Patton's favorite psalm? Why?

We gain more
by letting our real selves to be seen,
than by pretending to be what we are not.
                François de la Rochefoucauld

IV

Poetry of the Psalms

God sent his Singers upon earth
With songs of sadness and of mirth,
That they might touch the hearts of men
And bring them back to heaven again.
Henry Wadsworth Longfellow

Unlike English poets, Hebrew poets
did not use sound rhyme.
Rather, they used thought rhyme,
which means they related two lines
in a variety of ways. Consider a few examples.

First, Hebrew poets related two lines
by repeating the idea of the first line
in the second line. Thus, the two lines
matched like a pair of shoes.
Take Psalm 144:4:

We are like a puff of wind;
our days are like a passing shadow.

Take also Psalm 55:5:

I am gripped by fear and trembling;
I am overcome with horror.

A second way Hebrew poets related two lines
was by contrasting
the thought of the first line
with the thought of the second line.
Take Psalm 30:5:

Tears may flow in the night,
but joy comes in the morning.

Take also Psalm 37:21:

The wicked
borrow and never pay back,
but good people
are generous with their gifts.

Finally, Hebrew poets related two lines
by beginning a thought in the first line
and completing it in the second line.
Take Psalm 127:1:

If the LORD does not protect the city,
it does no good for the sentries to stand guard.

Take also Psalm 118:9:

It is better to trust in the LORD
than to depend on human leaders.

The two lines are like two lovers;
one without the other is incomplete.

Needless to say, thought rhyme
is not the only device that Hebrew poets used.
But it dramatizes an important point.
Hebrew poetry is subtle.
It reveals itself to the prayerful meditator.
It conceals itself from the casual reader.

Journal

PRAYER AND PRESENCE–5

*Again, the starting point for serious meditation
is opening oneself
to an awareness of God's presence—
should God wish to give it.
Another procedure for doing this is "sensing."
The procedure is simple.*

I close my eyes, relax my body,
and "sense" three things:
1. my clothes embracing my arms, shoulders,
   waist, and legs,
2. my chair supporting my body, and
3. the floor supporting my feet.

After about twenty seconds of "sensing,"
I open my eyes and pray:

"My God, you embrace me as intimately
as the clothes I wear embrace my body.
May each sensation I feel
deepen my awareness of your loving presence
as I begin my prayer."

Then I begin my meditation,
following the usual "Daily Meditation Format."

*This week I will begin each meditation
by using the "sensing" procedure.*

O God, protect me from cowardly slander.

The truly dangerous enemy is the one
who appears outwardly as a friend.
Such an enemy feigns friendship,
but from a heart that is far from friendly.
The truly dangerous enemy is the one
who never engages in open confrontation,
but shoots arrows of slander and lies
from ambush. Against such a foe,
even the strong are often helpless.
David knew how to battle "outside" enemies,
but battling "inside" ones was more difficult.
Ancient Jews saw Psalm 64
as a reflection of David's state of mind
against cowardly, "inside" enemies.

God—listen to my prayer! . . .
Protect me . . . from mobs of evil people.
They sharpen their tongues like swords. . . .
They are quick to spread their
shameless lies; they destroy good people
with cowardly slander. . . .
But God shoots his arrows at them,
and suddenly they are wounded. He will
destroy them because of those words. . . .
All righteous people will rejoice. 1–4, 7–8, 10

How do I handle "inside" enemies?

A truth that's told with bad intent
Beats all the lies you can invent.
William Blake

Journal

Journal

O God, everything shouts and sings for joy.

A drought struck Israel.
The soil-dependent people feared the worst.
One by one the watercourses went dry.
The specter of famine hung over the land.
Prayers went up to God day and night.
Then it happened.
The rains came just in time.
Then one morning the farmers looked out
across the lush green fields
and sang a song of thanksgiving to God.

[O God,]
you send abundant rain on the plowed fields
and soak them with water;
you soften the soil with showers
and cause the young plants to grow.
What a rich harvest your goodness provides!
Wherever you go there is plenty.
The pastures are filled with flocks;
the hillsides are full of joy.
The fields are covered with sheep;
the valleys are full of wheat.
Everything shouts and sings for joy.   10–13

When do I sing for joy as the farmers did?

"Look at us," said the violets
blooming at her feet. "All last winter
we slept in seeming death . . .
but at the right time God awakened us,
and here we are to comfort you."   Edward Payson Roe

O God, how wonderful are the things you do.

Ardis Whitman
describes a musician who lived in her city.
One summer day he and his wife climbed up
the tower erected at the peak of Mohawk Trail
in the Berkshire Mountains.
He was so moved by the beauty of the scene
that he ran back to his car, got his cornet,
climbed back up the tower,
and began playing with all his heart—
for his own joy, the delight of tourists,
and the glory of God.

Praise God with shouts of joy, all people!
Sing to the glory of his name. . . .
Say to God,
"How wonderful are the things you do! . . .
Everyone on earth worships you;
they sing praises to you,
they sing praises to your name."
Come and see what God has done,
his wonderful acts among people. . . .
Come and listen, all who honor God, and I
will tell you what he has done for me.   1–5, 16

How and when does the Spirit move me
to give glory to God as the musician did?

Music expresses
that which cannot be said in words
and about which it is impossible to be silent.
                                        Victor Hugo

Psalm 67 Day four

O God, may all people everywhere honor you.

General George Washington
issued this decree to his army in 1777:
"Tomorrow being the day
set apart by the Honorable Congress
for public Thanksgiving and Praise;
and duty calling us devoutly to express
our grateful acknowledgments to God
for the manifold blessings he has granted us.
The General directs that the army remain
in its present quarters,
and that the Chaplains perform divine service
with their several Corps and brigades."
One of the psalms used by chaplains
at the services was, undoubtedly, Psalm 67.

God, be merciful to us and bless us;
look on us with kindness,
so that the whole world may know your will;
so that all nations may know your salvation.
May the peoples praise you, O God;
may all the peoples praise you! . . .
The land has produced its harvest;
God, our God, has blessed us.
God has blessed us;
may all people everywhere honor him. 1–3, 6–7

How do I give personal thanksgiving to God?

Happy are they who grieve not
for what they have not, but give thanks
for what they do have. Author unknown

Journal

O God, how glad we are to be in your presence.

The cloud is a prominent symbol
of God's presence in the Bible.
For example, God told Moses at Mount Sinai,
"I will come to you in a thick cloud,
so that the people will hear me speaking
with you and will believe you" (Exodus 19:9).
A cloud also led the Israelites
across the trackless desert (Exodus 13:21).
A cloud filled the Jerusalem Temple
after the Ark was brought to it (1 Kings 8:10).
Finally, the cloud symbol is prominent
in the Psalms. Take Psalm 68:

Sing to God,
sing praises to his name; prepare a way
for him who rides on the clouds.
His name is the LORD—
be glad in his presence! . . . With his many
thousands of mighty chariots the Lord comes
from Sinai into the holy place. . . .
Sing to God, kingdoms of the world,
sing praise to the Lord,
to him who rides in the sky. . . .
Proclaim God's power; his majesty is over Israel,
his might is in the skies.   4, 17, 32–34

Where do I experience God's presence most?

Nature is too thin a screen;
the glory of the omnipresent God
bursts through everywhere.   Ralph Waldo Emerson

Journal

Journal

O God, don't hide yourself, but come and save me.

Albert Schweitzer left the concert stage
in Europe, became a medical doctor,
opened a hospital, and served Africa's poor
until he died at the age of ninety. He wrote:

"Out here millions and millions
live without help or hope of it.
Every day thousands and thousands
endure the most terrible sufferings,
though medical science could avert them.
Every day there prevails
in many and many a far-off hut
a despair which we could banish. . . .
It is time we . . . face our responsibilities."
The cry of the ancient Hebrew in Psalm 69
applies equally to the modern African.

I am worn out from calling for help,
and my throat is aching.
I have strained my eyes, looking for your help. . . .
Answer me, LORD,
in the goodness of your constant love;
in your great compassion turn to me!
Don't hide yourself from your servant;
I am in great trouble. . . .
Come to me and save me.   3, 16–18

What I can do to help?

Only eyes washed by tears see clearly.
Louis L. Mann

O God, I am weak and poor; hurry to my aid.

A missionary writes from Africa:
"Many of the children miss school . . .
because they have to go to the woods
to search for food."
Protracted hunger in tiny children
causes the belly to swell, hair to turn gray,
and skin to crack.
Africans call this condition *kwashiorkor.*
It is the sickness the old baby gets
when the new baby comes, because there is
no mother's milk left for the old baby.
Could the old baby speak,
its cries might echo Psalm 70.

*Save me, O God! L*ORD*, help me now! . . .*
I am weak and poor; come to me quickly,
*O God. You are my savior and my L*ORD*—*
hurry to my aid!   1, 5

What are my thoughts as I imagine
I am an African parent whose old baby
suffers from *kwashiorkor?*

It is easy enough to tell the poor
to accept their poverty as God's will
when you yourself have warm clothes
and plenty of food and medical care . . .
but if you want them to believe you—
try to share some of their poverty and see
if you can accept it as God's will yourself.
Thomas Merton, *Seeds of Contemplation*

Journal

When the people read it,
they were filled with joy.
Acts 15:31

PRAYER AND READING–1

One popular procedure for praying
involves four phases:
reading, thinking, speaking, listening.
Consider the reading *phase.*
Three guidelines should be observed.

———————

First, I do not read the meditation as I would
a magazine or a book. I read it more
as I would read a love letter from God to me.
Second, I read it slowly,
pausing momentarily after each sentence.
This allows time for the thought
of the sentence to sink in.

Sometimes reading in a low voice
makes the experience
more intimate and prayerful.
Third, when I have finished reading
the entire meditation,
I pick out some thought, feeling, or idea
that struck me during the reading.
This becomes the bridge
to the *thinking* phase of my prayer,
which will be dealt with in Week 13.

This week I will follow the above guidelines
during the reading phase of my meditation.

O God, you sent me troubles, but you also strengthened me.

Bobby Allyson, a stock car legend,
compiled an amazing win record.
Then Bobby's fortunes reversed abruptly.
A crash at Pocono International Raceway
ended his career, almost killing him.
A few years later his youngest son
was killed in the Busch Grand National.
Eleven months later his remaining son
was killed in a copter crash in Alabama.
Finally, his friend Neil Bonner was killed
just before the 1994 Daytona 500.
Inside Sports asked Bobby how he was able
to accept the tragedies so calmly.
Bobby said, "My faith has helped me,
because I can get down on my knees
and turn to God for strength."

My life has been an example to many,
because you have been my strong defender.
All day long I praise you
and proclaim your glory. . . .
You have sent troubles and suffering on me,
but you will restore my strength. . . .
You will make me greater than ever;
you will comfort me again.   7–8, 20–21

What questions about his faith
might I ask Allyson?

Feed your faith, and your doubts
will starve to death.   E. C. McKenzie

Journal

Journal

O God, help the needy and defeat their oppressors.

Just before his second term,
President Harry Truman wrote the following
in a note to his daughter, Margaret:
"Your dad
will never be reckoned among the great.
But you can be sure he did his level best
and gave all he had to his country.
There's an epitaph
in Boothill Cemetery in Tombstone, Arizona,
which reads,
'Here lies Jack Williams;
He done his damndest.'
What more can a person do?"
The psalmist prays that Israel's king
will be this kind of a dedicated leader.

Teach the king
to judge with your righteousness, O God;
share with him your own justice. . . .
May the king judge the poor fairly;
may he help the needy
and defeat their oppressors. . . .
May the king's name never be forgotten. . . .
May all nations ask God to bless them
as he has blessed the king.   1, 4, 17

What keeps me from being a more dedicated
leader at home? On the job?

When the czar has a cold, all Russia coughs.
Russian proverb

O God, you are all I need and all I want.

Saint Augustine and his mother, Monica,
went to a rural area for a short vacation.
He writes: "The two of us . . .
were discussing what it would be like
to share the eternal life
that the saints in heaven now enjoyed."
During the discussion,
the world's pleasures paled and Psalm 73
took on new meaning. In Psalm 73
the psalmist is concerned—even bitter—
that evil people prosper. He writes:

I tried to think this problem through,
but it was too difficult for me until I went
into your Temple. Then I understood
what will happen to the wicked. . . .
They go down to a horrible end. . . .
At the end you will receive me with honor.
What else do I have in heaven but you?
Since I have you,
what else could I want on earth?
16–17, 19, 24–25

What questions might I ask Augustine
and his mother?
What responses might they give me?

"What no one ever saw or heard,
what no one ever thought could happen,
is the very thing God prepared
for those who love him." 1 Corinthians 2:9

Journal

Journal

O God, why have you abandoned us like this?

The destruction of Jerusalem and the Temple in 586 B.C.E. shook the faith of God's people to the very foundations.
It triggered a series of agonizing, terrifying questions.

Why have you abandoned us like this, O God?
Will you be angry
with your own people forever?
Remember your people. . . .
Remember Mount Zion, where you once lived.
Walk over these total ruins; our enemies
have destroyed everything in the Temple. . . .
They smashed all the wooden panels
with their axes and sledge hammers.
They wrecked your Temple and set it on fire;
they desecrated the place
where you are worshiped. . . .
All our sacred symbols are gone;
there are no prophets left,
and no one knows how long this will last. . . .
Why have you refused to help us?
Why do you keep your hands behind you?
1–3, 6–7, 9, 11

What are my thoughts as I imagine
I am an ancient Jew sitting near the Temple,
weeping at what I see? What is my prayer?

Rouse yourself, God, and defend your cause!
Psalm 74:22

O God, you have set a time for judgment.

Journal

C. S. Lewis was riding on a bus.
Suddenly a disturbing thought came to him.
He was keeping a door shut on something.
Moreover, he felt at that moment that he
was being given a graced opportunity—
either to open the door or to keep it shut.
He chose to open it. He says:
"For the first time I examined myself
with a serious practical purpose.
And there I found what appalled me;
a zoo of lusts, a bedlam of ambitions, . . .
a harem of fondled hatreds."   *Surprised by Joy*
All of us can relate to such "crisis moments"
when God floods us with light and graces us
with power to make a choice—
to face the sun and walk into the light or
turn away from it and walk in the darkness.
Upon these moments we will be judged.

"I have set a time for judgment," says God,
"and I will judge with fairness. . . .
I tell the wicked not to be arrogant;
I tell them to stop their boasting."
Judgment does not come from the east
or from the west, from the north or from
the south; it is God who is the judge.   2, 4–7

What door may I be keeping shut? Why?

"[People] look at the outward appearance,
but I look at the heart."   1 Samuel 16:7

Journal

O God, how glorious you are! How majestic!

Helen Dukas and Banesh Hoffmann wrote a book called *Albert Einstein: The Human Side.*
They quote the great scientist as saying:
"Everyone who is seriously involved
in the pursuit of science becomes convinced
that a spirit is manifested
in the laws of the Universe—
a Spirit vastly superior to that of man,
and one in the face of which we
with our modest powers must feel humble."
Psalm 76 celebrates the power of God
and the folly of those who would oppose it.

How glorious you are, O God! How majestic,
as you return from the mountains
where you defeated your foes.
Their brave soldiers
have been stripped of all they had
and now are sleeping the sleep of death;
all their strength and skill was useless. . . .
No one can stand in your presence
when you are angry. . . .
The world was afraid and kept silent,
when you rose up to pronounce judgment,
to save all the oppressed on earth.   4–5, 7–9

How do I visualize what the psalmist says?

If the psalmist delights in God the Warrior,
we can hardly blame him: it is only a child
boasting of his Father's strength.   Alexander Jones

When I think of you, O God, I sigh.

A teacher gave her students several psalms and asked them which one best expressed their present feelings.
One student chose Psalm 77, explaining: "Somewhere in grade school my ideas of God underwent a big change. I found myself no longer taking God very seriously.
This attitude continued to stay with me until my second year in high school.
Then one Sunday, for a reason I can't explain, I decided to go to church—
something I hadn't done since grade school.
That Sunday I rediscovered God in my life."

I cannot find comfort.
When I think of God, I sigh; . . .
I feel discouraged.
He keeps me awake all night;
I am so worried that I cannot speak.
I think of days gone by. . . .
I spend the night in deep thought . . .
and this is what I ask myself:
"Will the Lord always reject us?
Will he never again be pleased with us?" 2–7

What could I say to God
about my absence from church and the reason
I returned—or should return?

If I walk one step toward God,
God will run ten steps toward me. Anonymous

PRAYER AND READING–2

Charles Laughton was reading Shakespeare's
Twelfth Night *to a group of English teachers.
Afterward a young teacher protested, saying,
"That wasn't quite fair. You edited
those passages to make them livelier."
"But I didn't skip a word," Laughton replied.
"Whatever made you think that I did?"
"Well," he said, "this was the first time
I ever completely understood the play."
Laughton said later, "I feel certain that
the teacher's new appreciation of the drama
was inspired by the enjoyment
of hearing it read."*

That story makes an important point.
Hearing something read—or reading it
out loud—heightens my appreciation of it.
Scientific experiment shows further
that when I both *see* and *hear* words read,
my ability to understand and remember them
is dramatically enhanced.

*This week I will read each meditation
slowly and reverently in a whisper
or a subdued voice.
I will also pause after each sentence
to allow its meaning to sink in.*

O God, you led your people with the light of a fire.

A young woman listened with astonishment
and crushing disappointment when the lawyer
read the will of her favorite aunt:
"To my favorite niece
I give my favorite possession, my Bible.
May she reap great rewards
from pondering God's word."
The niece was so crushed, she put the Bible
on a shelf and never bothered to open it.
Only when she gave it to the Salvation Army,
years later, did she learn that her aunt
had placed $5,000 within its pages.
Within the pages of the Bible is a vast treasure,
far greater than all the money in the world.
The psalmist refers to it this way:

*Listen, my people, to my teaching,
and pay attention to what . . . our ancestors
told us . . . about the LORD's power
and . . . the wonderful things he has done. . . .
He instructed our ancestors
to teach his laws to their children. . . .
In this way they also will put their trust in God
and not forget what he has done . . .
and . . . remain faithful to him.*   1, 3–5, 7–8

Why is the Bible such a treasure?

*The Bible is a window in this prison world,
through which we may look into eternity.*
Timothy Dwight

Journal

111

Journal

Help us, O God;
forgive our sins and save us.

The destruction of Jerusalem
and the desecration of the Temple
brought God's people to their knees.
They cried aloud in soul-deep anguish:

O God,
the heathen have invaded your land.
They have desecrated your holy Temple
and left Jerusalem in ruins.
They left the bodies of your people
for the vultures, the bodies of your servants
for wild animals to eat. . . .
No one was left to bury the dead. . . .
Help us, O God, and save us;
rescue us and forgive our sins
for the sake of your own honor. . . .
Listen to the groans of the prisoners,
and by your great power
free those who are condemned to die. . . .
Then we . . . , the sheep of your flock,
will thank you forever
and praise you for all time to come.   1–3, 9, 11, 13

How do I even begin to try to make sense
out of this momentous tragedy
that God let happen to the Chosen People?

What we suffer at this present time
cannot be compared at all
with the glory that is going to be
revealed to us.   Romans 8:18

Come and save
your people, O God.

After Solomon's death,
civil war split God's people into two groups:
the North, called Israel,
and the South, called Judah. In 722 B.C.E.,
Assyria invaded the North and enslaved it.
The psalmist weeps over the catastrophe
and cries out in sorrow and confusion:

Bring us back, O God! . . .
You have given us sorrow to eat,
a large cup of tears to drink. . . .
You brought a grapevine out of Egypt. . . .
It extended its branches . . .
as far as the Euphrates River.
Why did you break down the fences around it?
Now anyone passing by can steal its grapes;
wild hogs trample it down. . . .
Come and save this grapevine
that you planted. . . .
Our enemies have set it on fire. . . .
Bring us back, LORD God Almighty.
Show us your mercy, and we will be saved.
3, 5, 8, 11–13, 15–16, 19

As I visualize the plight of God's grapevine,
what parallel do I see between it
and the Church today?

It is impossible for the Church
to remain on its feet
if it doesn't get on its knees. Anonymous

Journal

O God, our God, you brought us out of Egypt.

"We are not innocent bystanders
in the cosmic drama.
There is in us more kinship with the divine
than we are able to believe.
Our souls are candles of the Lord,
lit on the cosmic way, rather than the fireworks
produced by the combustion
of nature's explosive compositions,
and every soul is indispensable to Him.
We are needed; each of us is a hand of God."
Rabbi Abraham Heschel (slightly adapted)

I hear an unknown voice saying,
"I took the burdens off your backs;
I let you put down your loads of bricks.
When you were in trouble, you called to me,
and I saved you.
From my hiding place in the storm,
I answered you. . . .
Listen, my people, to my warning;
Israel, how I wish you would listen to me!
You must never worship another god.
I am the LORD your God,
who brought you out of Egypt." 5–10

How do I understand "candles of the Lord,
lit on the cosmic way," "a hand of God,"
"an unknown voice," "hiding place in the storm"?

God loves man's lamplight better than
his own great stars. Rabindranath Tagore

God says, "Rescue the needy and the helpless."

The Mountain People is a disturbing book
about the Ik, a vanishing African tribe.
Driven from their hunting grounds,
they are barely surviving.
Food is so scarce that young people
steal from the mouths of the elderly.
Along with the sick and the weak,
the elderly are simply left to die.
Colin Turnbull, the author of the book,
detects a parallel between
the situation of the Ik and the West.
Like the Ik, we have opted for the road
of individualism.
Our primary driving force
is our own self-interest.
Turnbull ends his book on a chilling note:
"Is the sorry plight of the Ik
a preview of our own future?"

Defend the rights of the poor and the orphans;
be fair to the needy and the helpless.
Rescue them
from the power of evil people.   3–4

What can I do to help rescue the poor,
the needy, and the helpless from evil powers?

An age is called Dark,
not because the light fails to shine,
but because people refuse to see it.
James Michener

Journal

115

Psalm 83 Day six

Journal

O God, do not keep silent; do not be still.

The Holocaust in Nazi Germany in the 1940s caused many modern Jews to cry out to God, "Where are you? Don't you see our tears? Can't you hear our cries? Don't you see what's happening to us?" But no answer came. God remained silent. Ancient Jews experienced a similar crisis on several occasions. God did not respond to their cries, and they shouted in anguish:

O God, do not keep silent;
do not be still . . . ! Look! Your enemies . . .
form an alliance against you. . . .
Scatter them like dust, O God,
like straw blown away by the wind.
As fire burns the forest,
as flames set the hills on fire,
chase them away . . . with your fierce winds.
Cover their faces with shame, O LORD. . . .
May they be defeated and terrified. . . .
May they know that you alone
are the LORD.   1–2, 5, 13–18

As I reread the two above descriptions, imagining myself to be the victim in each, why do I think God remains silent at certain times in our lives?

God's silence
ripens man's thoughts into speech.
Rabindranath Tagore, *Stray Birds*

O God, even the sparrows nest near your altars.

A man was walking past
the Church of the Little Flower
in Royal Oak, Michigan.
He glanced up at the huge crucifix
on the front of the church.
There he saw several sparrows
dancing about on the shoulder of Jesus.
Looking closer, he saw that they had built
a nest between the shoulder of Jesus
and the horizontal bar of the cross.
He says this happy image always returns
when he reads Psalm 84.

How I love your Temple, LORD Almighty!
How I want to be there!
I long to be in the LORD's Temple.
With my whole being I sing for joy
to the living God.
Even the sparrows have built a nest . . .
near your altars, LORD Almighty. . . .
How happy are those who live in your Temple,
always singing praise to you.
How happy are those whose strength
comes from you, . . . who trust in you!   1–5, 12

How deeply do I yearn for the presence
of the living God?

Jacob woke up and said, "The LORD is here!
He is in this place, and I didn't know it!"
Genesis 28:16

Journal

Problem Psalms

A tourist pointed to an old wagon
in a deserted western mining town and said,
"Look at the wreck! Can you believe
that people actually rode
in primitive contraptions like that?"

It is a tragic mistake to judge the past
by the standards of the present.
One area where that is frequently done
is in the Hebrew psalms.

For example,
modern Christians often criticize them
for their "vengeful" tone and language.
Take Psalm 58:8.
The psalmist cries out in anguish
concerning evil people:

May they be like snails
that dissolve into slime;
may they be like a baby born dead
that never sees the light.

When we read lines like these,
we need to keep in mind
that they were written at a time
when Israel had no clear idea
of life after death.

The concept of reward and punishment
in an afterlife did not emerge
until the second century B.C.E.,
and then it was seen only in vague terms.

Thus the psalmist assumed
that God would punish evil people
and reward good people in this life.
Seen in this light,
the psalmist's prayer for vengeance
was in reality a cry for justice.

We must also keep in mind
that Israel's early ideas of God were primitive.
Only with the passage of time
and with more revelation
did their ideas of God develop and mature.

Although the Book of Psalms
was edited after Israel's concept of God
had passed beyond some of the earlier ideas
expressed in the psalms,
the editor was inspired to preserve them.

There is an honesty here that is appealing.
By including these psalms,
the editor provided a yardstick
that enables us to measure
how Israel's idea of God evolved and matured
over the passage of centuries.

Journal

Mary remembered
all these things
and thought deeply about them.
Luke 2:19

PRAYER AND THINKING

A student wrote: "I came home one night
and turned on the TV to watch the news.
It was a typical Chicago day:
robbery, murder, and rape. It seemed as if
someone had called time-out on good news.
I cut the tube and sat in the dark, thinking,
'Why are we doing this? Where is God?
If God loves us so much, why is all this going on?'
I became deeply depressed.
For the first time in a long time,
I found myself praying with all my being."

The student's experience illustrates
the *thinking* phase of prayer.

To use a biblical example, it is doing
what Mary did after the shepherds told her
what the angel had said concerning Jesus.
Mary "thought deeply" about their words.
During the thinking phase of prayer
I think "deeply" about what I have just read
and let my thoughts become a springboard
to the third phase of prayer:
the *speaking* phase.

This week I will do what Mary did.
I will think "deeply" about what I read
in each meditation.

O God, you promise to bless us and stay with us.

Dale Carnegie describes a farewell dinner
for people who had just completed his course
in public speaking.
Dozens of participants took turns
eulogizing a retiring colleague.
One speaker's words stood out.
With eyes and voice filled with emotion,
he turned to his friend and said:
"I touch my heart as the Easterns do;
May the peace of Allah abide with you.
Wherever you come, wherever you go,
May the beautiful palms of Allah grow.
Through days of labor and nights of rest,
May the love of Allah make you blest.
I touch my heart as the Easterns do;
May the peace of Allah abide with you."
Author unknown

It is this kind of precious blessing
of peace and abiding presence
that Psalm 85 speaks of when it says:

The LORD God . . . promises peace to us, . . .
and his saving presence
will remain in our land.   8–9

When did I last thank or pray for
someone who helped me very much?

[Laban said to Jacob,] "May the LORD
keep an eye on us while we are separated
from each other." Genesis 31:49

Journal

Journal

Listen to me, O God; I pray to you all day long.

A young person, imprisoned in Argentina for espousing the cause of the poor against the government, said after being released: "What characterized our Christian life during this whole time in prison was prayer, more precisely, prayer of intercession. When you hear the despairing screams of your friends who are all in the process of being tortured, and when you experience your total helplessness to do anything, you learn that to pray and to intercede with God is the only worthy human act that one is capable of doing."

Listen to me, LORD, and answer me,
for I am helpless and weak. . . .
I am your servant and I trust in you.
You are my God, so be merciful to me;
I pray to you all day long. . . .
Listen, LORD, to my prayer;
hear my cries for help.
I call to you in times of trouble,
because you answer my prayers. . . .
Turn to me and have mercy on me;
strengthen me and save me.   1–3, 6–7, 16

What role does the prayer of intercession play in my life?

The best prayers have often been
more groans than words.   John Bunyan

O God, you built your city on your sacred hill.

Journal

God blessed the Jewish people,
calling them "my people" (Psalm 81:8).
God blessed the city of Jerusalem,
making it the "city of God" (Psalm 87:3).
God blessed the Temple of Jerusalem,
making it the "house of God" (Matthew 12:4).
The psalmist sees these as the foundation
for a "greater blessing" for all peoples.

The LORD built his city on the sacred hill;
more than any other place in Israel
he loves the city of Jerusalem.
Listen, city of God, to the wonderful things
he says about you. . . .
Of Zion it will be said
that all nations belong there
and that the Almighty will make her strong.
The LORD will write a list of the peoples
and include them all as citizens of Jerusalem.
They dance and sing,
"In Zion is the source of all our blessings."   1–3, 5–7

How can I relate this to Augustine's words:
"In the Old Testament the New is concealed;
in the New Testament the Old is revealed"?

I saw the Holy City, the new Jerusalem,
coming down out of heaven from God. . . .
I heard a loud voice speaking from the throne:
"Now God's home is with people! . . .
There will be no more death."   Revelation 21:2–4

O God, I am in deep trouble with no way out.

Meryl Streep won an Oscar for her portrayal
of a young mother in *Sophie's Choice*.
A meditation on evil, the story is set in Brooklyn
in the late 1940s. It is told by Stingo,
who falls in love with Sophie
and learns her tragic story.
During the war she had been sent to Auschwitz,
a death camp, with her two little children.
There she was told she must give them up.
One would be sent to a children's camp;
the other would be taken to the gas chamber.
The inhumane choice forced upon Sophie
(which child would die) destroys her—
spiritually and psychologically.
Psalm 88 mirrors the guilt and despair
that swallow her up after her decision.

[LORD God,] all my strength is gone. . . .
You have thrown me into the depths
of the tomb, into the darkest and deepest pit.
Your anger lies heavy on me,
and I am crushed beneath its waves. . . .
I am closed in and cannot escape.   4, 6–8

If Sophie poured out her tragic story to me
and asked me to help her deal with it,
what would I say to her—of evil, love, God?

There is some soul of goodness in things evil,
Would men observingly distil it out.
William Shakespeare, *Henry IV*

O God, you have taken away his royal scepter.

In 1981 Solidarity grew from
a labor movement in the shipyards of Gdansk
to a political revolution in the Polish nation.
For seventeen intoxicating months,
Poland defied the might of Russia.
Then came the night of December 12, 1982.
With 100,000 Soviet troops massed on the border
and with orders from the Kremlin,
Polish General Jaruzelski silenced all phones.
Tanks rolled into all major cities,
and armed troops beat back coal miners.
At three in the morning,
police broke into the home of Lech Walesa,
the revolution's leader, and arrested him.
Suddenly all of Poland was thrown
into an abyss. Their tragic situation
mirrored Israel's situation centuries before.

[LORD!] In a vision long ago you said . . . ,
"I have made my servant David king. . . .
I will crush his foes. . . ."
But you are angry with your chosen king. . . .
You have taken away his royal scepter
and knocked his throne to the ground. . . .
How long will your anger burn like fire?
19–20, 23, 38, 44, 46

What lesson might this parallel hold for me?

History is an early warning system.
Norman Cousins

Journal

Teach us, O God, how short is our life.

Abraham Lincoln told this story in a speech.
An Eastern king charged his wise men
to compose a sentence, "to be ever in view,
and which should be true and appropriate
in all times and situations." After much thought
the wise men wrote this sentence:
"And this, too, shall pass away."
Lincoln then made this insightful comment:
"How chastening in the hour of pride!
How consoling in the depth of affliction."
Lincoln's story recalls Psalm 90.

[O LORD,] you were eternally God. . . .
A thousand years to you are like one day;
they are like yesterday, already gone. . . .
We are like weeds that sprout in the morning,
that grow and burst into bloom,
then dry up and die in the evening. . . .
Teach us how short our life is,
so that we may become wise. 2, 4–6, 12

How do the story and the psalm speak to me?

A good leg will fall. A straight back will stoop.
A black beard will turn white. . . .
A curled pate will grow bald. . . .
But a good heart . . .
shines bright and never changes.

Vice President Walter Mondale eulogized
deceased Vice President Hubert Humphrey
in these words adapted from Shakespeare's *Henry V.*

O God, in you
I put all my trust.

The famous actor Jimmy Stewart was a pilot
in World War II. Before he left for combat,
his father slipped this note into his pocket:
"Dear Jim, Soon after you read this letter,
you will be on your way to the worst sort
of danger. . . . I am banking on the enclosed
copy of Psalm 91. The thing that takes the place
of fear and worry is the promise
of these words. . . .
I love you more than I can tell you. Dad."

Whoever goes to the LORD for safety,
whoever remains under the protection
of the Almighty, can say to him,
"You are my defender and protector.
You are my God; in you I trust." . . .
He will cover you with his wings;
you will be safe in his care. . . .
A thousand may fall dead beside you,
ten thousand all around you,
but you will not be harmed.   1–2, 4, 7

How might I deepen my faith in God?

God says, "I will save those who love me
and will protect those
who acknowledge me as LORD.
When they call to me, I will answer them;
when they are in trouble,
I will be with them . . . [and] rescue them."
                Psalm 91:14–15

The LORD said, "I was ready
to answer my people's prayers,
but they did not pray."
Isaiah 65:1

PRAYER AND SPEAKING–1

In his book Sadhana,
*Anthony de Mello tells about someone
who had been bedfast for many years.
The person was finding it very hard to pray
with any degree of attention.
One day a friend suggested
that he place an empty chair near the bed
and imagine Jesus to be sitting on it.
Then he told him to speak to Jesus,
just as the two of them were doing now.
The sick man tried it and it worked.*

That story makes an important point.
Often I can enhance the *speaking* phase
of meditation by imagining Jesus
to be seated or standing across from me.
I do not spend time trying to picture
what Jesus looks like.
I simply sense his presence, as two people
in a dark room sense each other's presence.
Of course, Jesus is not sitting on the chair.
But Jesus is present. De Mello's suggestion
simply helps me "realize" and "localize"
this great mystery.

*This week I will experiment with
de Mello's "empty chair" suggestion.*

O God, if we live by your light, we will always bear fruit.

Author Stephen McKenna says,
"There are trees
that are all a-strain upward like a prayer;
there are trees that rise only to flow
eternally downwards, drooping like death . . .
but in all trees there is beauty."
The psalmist agreed.
He liked to compare a good person to a tree.
We see this in Psalm 1 and here in Psalm 92.
The most celebrated trees in biblical times
were the great cedars of Lebanon.
They attained diameters of thirteen feet.
Their wood was used to panel the inner walls
of the Jerusalem Temple. The psalmist sings:

The righteous will flourish like palm trees;
they will grow like the cedars of Lebanon.
They are like trees
planted in the house of the LORD,
that flourish in the Temple of our God,
that still bear fruit in old age
and are always green and strong.   12–14

Jesus was also fond of the tree image.
He compared people to trees,
some bearing good fruit, others bad (Matthew 12:33).
What are some concrete examples
of the fruit my life is bearing right now?

Hell is truth seen too late—
duty neglected in its season.   Tyron Edwards

Journal

O God, your power exceeds that of the sea.

The "royal psalms" relate to Israel's kings.
Starting with David,
the kings become earthly images of God,
who reigns serenely
from a heavenly throne over all of creation.
Psalm 93 contrasts two striking images:
the serene God and the roaring sea.

The LORD is king.
He is clothed with majesty and strength.
The earth is set firmly in place
and cannot be moved.
Your throne, O LORD,
has been firm from the beginning,
and you existed before time began.
The ocean depths raise their voice, O LORD;
they raise their voice and roar.
The LORD rules supreme in heaven,
greater than the roar of the ocean,
more powerful
than the waves of the sea. 1–4

How is Psalm 93 related prophetically
to the storm at sea—
where a calm, serene "Jesus stood up
and commanded the wind, 'Be quiet!' and he said
to the waves, 'Be still!' The wind died down,
and there was a great calm" (Mark 4:39)?

Jesus said [to Pilate], "My kingdom
does not belong to this world." John 18:36

O God, you will not abandon us; justice will return again.

A bumper sticker reads,
"Stop the world; I want to get off!"
It echoes the feeling of many people
in the face of mounting crime and
exploitation of the poor and the powerless.
The psalmist echoes the same feeling but,
at the same time, affirms that God is in control
and will act at the appropriate time.

LORD, you are a God who punishes. . . .
You are the judge of us all;
rise and give the proud what they deserve!
How much longer will the wicked be glad?
How much longer, LORD?
How much longer will criminals be proud
and boast about their crimes?
They crush your people, LORD;
they oppress those who belong to you. . . .
They say, "The LORD does not see us;
the God of Israel does not notice.". . .
The LORD will not abandon his people. . . .
Justice will again be found in the courts,
and all righteous people will support it.
1–5, 7, 14–15

What one crime would I like to see stopped
in the world—and why?

We'll never stop crime
until we get over the idea that we can
hire or elect people to stop it.   Anonymous

Journal

Journal

O God, we kneel before you, our Lord and Maker.

Has not every person, at one time,
climbed a grassy hill and contemplated
the quilt of fields and forests and asked,
"Why all this? What secret does it hold?
Why the new calf walking with its mother?
Why the sun warming plowed fields?
Why the buttercups bobbing in the breeze?
Why the world—birthing, growing, dying?
What secret does it hold?"
And hardly has the question formed,
when stems of grass and blades of wheat
point skyward—short of telling the secret.
But what they say is more than sufficient.

Come, let us praise the LORD! . . .
He rules over the whole earth,
from the deepest caves to the highest hills.
He rules over the sea, which he made;
the land also, which he himself formed.
Come, let us bow down and worship him;
let us kneel before the LORD, our Maker!
He is our God;
we are the people he cares for.   1, 4–7

What questions might I ask God
about the beauty of nature?

It is our destiny to ponder the riddle
of existence and, as a by-product of our
wonderment, create a new life on earth.
Charles Kettering

O God, all the world proclaims your glory.

David brought the Ark of the Covenant to Jerusalem and placed it in a sacred tent. Then he appointed Levites (priestly tribe of the Israelites) to lead daily worship services in the tent. These services included the use of "trumpets and cymbals and the other instruments which were played when the songs of praise were sung" (1 Chronicles 16:42). Among the "songs of praise" that the Levites sang was Psalm 96.

Sing a new song to the LORD!
Sing to the LORD, all the world! . . .
Proclaim every day the good news
that he has saved us.
Proclaim his glory to the nations,
his mighty deeds to all peoples. . . .
The gods of all other nations are only idols,
but the LORD created the heavens. . . .
Praise the LORD's glorious name;
bring an offering and come into his Temple.
Bow down before the Holy One.   1–3, 5, 8–9

What are my thoughts as I imagine entering the sacred tent late at night to speak to God?

Time doesn't enfold God;
space can't hold God.
Intelligence can't grasp God.
Imagination can't conceive God.
Absolutely nothing is like God.   Abdallah Ibn Tumart

Journal

133

Psalm 97

Journal

O God, clouds surround you and fire goes in front of you.

"In flights of wild fantasy,
I've streaked across the sky,
tunneled the clouds and touched the stars.
In daring flights of ecstasy
I've fled my craft,
danced on the wind,
and painted rainbows in the sky.
I've stowed away on meteors,
explored the Milky Way—
planted my own flag on the moon.
I've talked with eagles
and followed flights of birds
to worlds you've never dreamed of.
Laughing in symphony with thunder,
and skipping rope with lightning bolts,
I've fled my skin and walked with God."   M. L.

The LORD is king! Earth, be glad!
Rejoice, you islands of the seas!
Clouds . . . surround him. . . .
Fire goes in front of him. . . .
His lightning lights up the world . . .
and all the nations see his glory.   1–4, 6

How have I experienced fleeing my skin
and walking with God?

Walking with God
isn't a matter of the intellect.
It's a matter of the heart.
Joni Eareckson Tada

O God, we clap our hands and sing for joy before you.

Elizabeth Starr Hill was vacationing
in Spain. She writes:
"Early every morning my young son
went to the balcony of our hotel
to see what kind of day it would be,
and every day it was the same—
inexhaustibly sunny—until one morning
I heard a whoop of joy and
the exultant words, 'Hurray! It's raining!'
Glorious to see the dusty streets and
rooftops running with rain.
Delightful to breathe the cleansed air,
to smell the wet earth!"
Longfellow's poem came to Hill's mind:
"How beautiful is the rain!
After the dust and heat,
In the broad and fiery street,
In the narrow lane,
How beautiful is the rain!"

Sing a new song to the LORD;
he has done wonderful things! . . .
Sing for joy to the LORD, all the earth. . . .
Roar, sea, and every creature in you;
sing, earth, and all who live on you!
Clap your hands, you rivers; you hills,
sing together with joy before the LORD.   1, 4, 7–8

What are my thoughts as I join the chorus?

God is, and all is well.   John Greenleaf Whittier

PRAYER AND SPEAKING–2

A student in a school prayer group was all excited. He said: "Last night I was home all alone. So I decided to pray out loud. It was overpowering. Then I stopped talking out loud and spoke silently to God in a way I've never been able to do before."

Possibly, I can appreciate
the student's excitement,
because I too have experienced the impact
that speaking out loud to God can have.
A reason for this impact is that it heightens
the reality that I am *speaking* to God.

Years ago, when Bill Moyers was press secretary under President Lyndon Johnson, he was saying grace one morning at breakfast. Suddenly, Lyndon interrupted him, saying, "Louder! Louder! I can't hear you." Without looking up, Moyers simply said, "I am not speaking to you, Mr. President!" And so speaking out loud in prayer heightens the fact that I am speaking to "someone." I am speaking to God.

This week during the speaking phase of my mediation I will speak to God out loud, in a subdued voice.

O God, you are holy, and all creation praises you.

Journal

Pilot John Magee Jr. wrote "High Flight"
on the back of a letter to his parents in 1941,
saying, "It started at 30,000 feet and was finished
soon after I landed." The poem reads:
"Oh! I have slipped the surly bonds of Earth
And danced the skies on laughter-silvered wings;
Sunward I've climbed, and joined
   the tumbling mirth
of sun-split clouds,—and done a hundred things
You have never dreamed of—
   wheeled and soared and swung
High in the sunlit silence. Hov'ring there,
I've chased the shouting wind along, and flung
My eager craft through footless halls of air. . . .

"Up, up the long, delirious burning blue
I've topped the wind-swept heights
   with easy grace
Where never lark nor ever eagle flew—
And, while with silent lifting mind I've trod
The high untrespassed sanctity of space,
Put out my hand, and touched the face of God."

The LORD . . . sits on his throne. . . .
Holy is he! . . . Praise the LORD our God. . . .
Holy is he! . . . The LORD our God is holy.   1, 3, 5, 9

When did I reach out and touch God's face?

"Holy, holy, holy! The LORD Almighty is holy!
His glory fills the world."   Isaiah 6:3

Journal

O God, we sing to you and worship you with joy.

One morning Robert Kyff was out jogging.
Suddenly he was stopped dead in his tracks
by the brilliant colors of an autumn tree.
As he jogged off, he thought of something
Ralph Waldo Emerson once said:
"If the stars came out
only one night each thousand years,
what great excitement that would generate.
But because they come out each night,
we pay little attention to them."
Kyff also recalled a story about
Emily Dickinson's father. One night he got
so excited over a display of the northern lights
that he rang the town's church bells.
He wanted everyone to come out
of their houses and savor the sight.
With similar excitement the psalmist invites
all peoples everywhere to worship God.

Sing to the LORD, all the world!
Worship the LORD with joy. . . .
Acknowledge that the LORD is God.
He made us, and we belong to him;
we are his people, we are his flock. . . .
Give thanks to him and praise him.
The LORD is good; his love is eternal.   1–5

What are my thoughts about creation?

The stars sang together, and
the heavenly beings shouted for joy.   Job 38:7

138

O God, I sing to you of loyalty and justice.

The winter of 1777 was an absolute nightmare for General George Washington and his army at Valley Forge. A staff officer described it in these words: "The unfortunate soldiers were in want of everything. The army frequently went for days without food, and the patient endurance of soldiers and officers was a miracle." Washington and his men drew strength from their faith in God. For example, Washington prayed Psalm 101 when he took command over his men.

My song is about loyalty and justice,
and I sing it to you, O LORD.
My conduct will be faultless. . . .
I will live a pure life in my house
and will never tolerate evil.
I hate the actions of those
who turn away from God . . .
and will have no dealings with evil.
I will get rid of anyone who whispers
evil things about someone else;
I will not tolerate anyone who is proud
and arrogant. . . . I will expel all
who are evil from the city of the LORD.   1–5, 8

How am I inspired by the faith of these giants?

I have the strength to face all conditions
by the power that Christ gives me.   Philippians 4:13

Journal

O God, don't take me away while I am still young.

John Quincy Adams, son of John Adams,
was the sixth president of the United States.
After his presidency, he returned to Congress.
Near the end of his career, he suffered a stroke.
Daniel Webster described
his final visit with Adams this way:
"A friend of his came in
and made a particular inquiry of his health.
Adams answered, 'I inhabit a weak, frail,
decayed tenement; battered by winds
and broken in upon by storms,
and from all I can learn,
the landlord doesn't intend to repair it.' "
Adams could relate to these words
of the psalmist:

My life is disappearing. . . .
I am beaten down like dry grass;
I have lost my desire for food. . . .
I am nothing but skin and bones. . . .
I lie awake;
I am like a lonely bird on a housetop. . . .
But you, O LORD, . . . you live forever. . . .
You are always the same,
and your life never ends.   3–5, 7, 12, 24, 27

What are my thoughts about growing old?

If wrinkles must be written upon brows,
let them not be written upon the heart.
The spirit should never grow old.   James Garfield

Journal

O God, your love is as high as the sky.

Years ago a tourist was sightseeing
along the back streets of a city in Iran.
He came upon a group of students
learning to weave rugs. After watching them
for a while, he said to one of them,
"What happens if you make a mistake?"
"Well," said the student, "our teacher
doesn't usually have us remove the mistake.
It would be too hard. He just takes over for a bit
and weaves it into his master pattern."
God does something similar when we sin.

Praise the LORD, my soul,
and do not forget how kind he is. . . .
He does not punish us as we deserve or
repay us according to our sins and wrongs.
As high as the sky is above the earth,
so great is his love for those who honor him.
As far as the east is from the west,
so far does he remove our sins from us.
As a father is kind to his children,
so the LORD is kind to those who honor him.
He knows what we are made of. . . .
Praise the LORD, my soul! 2, 10–14, 22

How do I experience God's kindness and mercy
to our world and to me, personally?

Among the attributes of God, although they
are all equal, mercy shines with even more brilliancy
than justice. Miguel de Cervantes

Journal

Psalm **104** Day six

O God, you ride on the wings of the wind.

Christina Rossetti was an invalid the last twenty years of her life, but this did not still the music in her soul. She writes:
"Who has seen the wind?
      Neither I nor you;
But when the leaves hang trembling
      The wind is passing through.
Who has seen the wind?
      Neither you nor I;
But when the trees bow down their heads
      The wind is passing by."
This poem recalls the Spirit and Psalm 104.

O LORD, my God, how great you are! . . .
You use the clouds as your chariot
and ride on the wings of the wind.
You use the winds as your messengers
and flashes of lightning as your servants.   1, 3–4

What can I say to express the music in my soul?

Breathe into me, Spirit of God,
that I may think what is holy.
Drive me, Spirit of God,
that I may do what is holy.
Draw me, Spirit of God,
that I may love what is holy.
Strengthen me, Spirit of God,
that I may preserve what is holy.
Guide me, Spirit of God,
that I may never lose what is holy.   Saint Augustine

Journal

O God, we tell the nations about your wonderful works.

King David appointed Asaph and the Levites
to conduct worship in the sacred tent
that he erected in the city of Jerusalem.
They prayed, offered sacrifice,
and sang "songs of praise" to the Lord
every morning and every night.
Among the songs that could be heard
echoing at sunrise and sunset from the tent
(forerunner to Temple) was Psalm 105.

Give thanks to the LORD,
proclaim his greatness;
tell the nations what he has done.
Sing praise to the LORD;
tell the wonderful things he has done.
Be glad that we belong to him;
let all who worship him rejoice.
Go to the LORD for help; and . . . remember
the miracles that God performed and
the judgments that he gave.
The LORD is our God;
his commands are for all the world.
He will keep his covenant forever,
his promises for a thousand generations.
1–4, 6–8

What could I say to name and
give thanks for some of the blessings
the Lord has given me?

What can I offer the LORD
for all his goodness to me?   Psalm 116:12

143

Pilgrim Psalms

Sidewalks were rare in Jesus' time.
There were footpaths, mostly, worn smooth
by thousands of feet passing over them.
These footpaths began to team with people
at the approach of the three major holidays
that Jews celebrated:
Passover, Pentecost, and Tabernacles.

People streamed out of small villages
to join larger groups for the long pilgrimage
to the Temple in Jerusalem.

One reason that people joined larger groups
was to protect themselves
from bands of roving outlaws (Luke 10:30).

Another reason for walking in larger groups
was for company and for entertainment.
To make the hours pass more quickly,
pilgrims sang psalms.
They could be heard for miles around
as their voices echoed from hillsides
and across fields.

A special medley of psalms was developed
for pilgrims to sing

on their journey to Jerusalem.
For example, there were special psalms
for the start of the journey, during it,
and when the Temple first came into view.

There were also special psalms to be sung
as they approached the gates of the city
and as they passed through the gates
and set foot inside it. Take Psalm 122:

I was glad when they said to me,
"Let us go to the Lord's house."
And now we are here,
standing inside the gates of Jerusalem!   1–2

Psalms 120–134 (NRSV) each contain notes
saying "A song of ascents."
Some scholars think these fifteen psalms
were among those that were sung
by the people in their ascent to Jerusalem.

We can imagine the excitement
with which Jesus sang these psalms
on his first trip to Jerusalem at age twelve.

Journal

PRAYER AND LISTENING

*A room was filled with applicants
for a single job as a telegraph operator.
Their voices competed with a flow
of dots and dashes from a telegraph key.
The door opened and a new applicant entered.
He listened for a minute, walked over
to a door marked "Private," and knocked.
A man opened it and said to the others,
"You may go; we are hiring this man."
When the others demanded an explanation,
the man at the door said, "Listen!"
The clicks of the key kept repeating,
"If you hear this, knock at the door
marked 'Private'; the job is yours."*

That story makes an important point.
God is constantly speaking to me,
but often I am simply not listening.
That is, God speaks to me through Scripture,
or an inspiring story, or an inspiring person,
but I do not pause and savor what I hear
so that it can take root in my heart and grow.

*This week I will make a special effort
to probe what I am reading,
pausing periodically to savor (listen to)
what God might be saying to me through it.*

O God, your people forgot you, but you didn't forget them.

The daily worship in the sacred tent
(future Temple) drew larger and larger crowds
each morning and each night.
One of the "worship songs"
that touched people's hearts was Psalm 106.
It contrasted Israel's infidelity to God
with God's fidelity to Israel.

Give thanks to the LORD,
because he is good; his love is eternal. . . .
Our ancestors in Egypt
did not understand God's wonderful acts. . . .
They forgot the God who had saved them
by his mighty acts in Egypt.
What wonderful things he did there!
What amazing things at the Red Sea! . . .
So the LORD was angry with his people;
he was disgusted with them.
He abandoned them
to the power of the heathen. . . .
Yet the LORD heard them when they cried. . . .
Let everyone say, "Amen!"   1, 7, 21–22, 40–41, 44, 48

As I imagine transporting myself in time
to one of the worship services in the sacred tent,
what do I experience
as I take a seat in the last row,
close my eyes, and simply *listen?*

Symphonies stretch your soul.
Paul Whiteman

Journal

O God, you calmed the storm and stilled the sea.

Alexander Selkirk was a Scottish sailor
who spent four years alone
on an uninhabited island in the south seas.
One day, near despair, he opened his Bible
randomly to Psalm 107. He read it
and it gave him new courage
to persevere until his rescue in 1708.

Some sailed over the ocean in ships,
earning their living on the seas. . . .
A mighty wind began to blow
and stirred up the waves.
The ships were lifted high in the air
and plunged down into the depths.
In such danger
the sailors lost their courage; . . .
all their skill was useless.
Then in their trouble they called to the LORD,
and he saved them from their distress.
He calmed the raging storm,
and the waves became quiet.   23, 25–29

What are my thoughts as I speak to Jesus
about the passage Selkirk read and *listen*
to what Jesus might say back to me?

[A storm blew up. The disciples shouted,]
"We are about to die!" Jesus got up and
gave an order to the wind . . . and there was
a great calm. Then he said to the disciples,
"Where is your faith?"   Luke 8:24–25

Your love and fidelity, O God, touch the skies.

In 1939 Hitler's armies were on the march.
England's survival looked bleak at best.
On Christmas Day,
King George VI addressed the nation
and counseled trust in God.
He ended by quoting from a poem
by Minnie Louise Haskins:
"I said to the man
who stood at the gate of the year:
'Give me a light
that I may tread safely into the unknown!'
And he replied: 'Go out into the darkness
and put your hand in the hand of God.
That shall be to you better than light
and safer than a known way.' "
The psalmist had a similar childlike trust.

[O LORD,] your constant love
reaches above the heavens;
your faithfulness touches the skies. . . .
Save us by your might; answer my prayer,
so that the people you love
may be rescued. . . .
Human help is worthless.
With God on our side we will win.   4, 6, 12–13

What are my thoughts as I speak to Jesus about
his trust in his Father and *listen* to his reply?

The more we depend on God,
the more dependable we find God is.   Cliff Richards

Journal

O God, evildoers may curse me, but you will bless me.

Marine Jimmy Lopez was held hostage
444 days by Iranian extremists.
Commenting on how the family coped
with the ordeal, his mother said:
"We put our trust in God.
When things got unbearable,
we talked with God the way Jesus did
in the Garden of Gethsemane."
Psalm 109 describes someone coping
with a similar ordeal in a similar way.
After venting feelings of anger and anguish,
the psalmist regains his perspective
and prays from the heart.

Help me, O LORD my God;
because of your constant love, save me!
Make my enemies know that you are the one
who saves me.
They may curse me, but you will bless me. . . .
I will give loud thanks to the LORD;
I will praise him in the assembly . . .
because he defends the poor and saves them
from those who condemn them.   26–28, 30–31

What are my thoughts as I speak to Jesus about
Jimmy and the psalmist and *listen* to his reply?

The LORD who created you says,
"Do not be afraid. . . .
When you pass through deep waters,
I will be with you."   Isaiah 43:1–2

O God, you made a promise and will not take it back.

God promised David that a Messiah
would come from his royal line of descendants.
Each coronation of a Davidic king, therefore,
occasioned a great celebration.
For each king meant that Israel was a step closer
to the Messiah, the "King of Kings."
Like all kings—starting with Melchizedek—
the Messiah's function would include
both *royal* and *priestly* duties (Genesis 14, 18–20).
This explains why early Christians saw
the priesthood of Melchizedek as pointing
to the priesthood of the Christ (Hebrews 7).
It also explains why Psalm 110 played
a prominent role in the coronation of kings.

The LORD said to my lord,
"Sit here at my right side
until I put your enemies under your feet.". . .
The LORD will extend your royal power. . . .
The LORD made a solemn promise
and will not take it back:
"You will be a priest forever
in the priestly order of Melchizedek."   1–2, 4

What are my thoughts as I speak to Jesus,
who was priest and victim of the sacrifice
he offered for our sins, and *listen* to his reply?

My saving power will rise on you
like the sun and bring healing
like the sun's rays.   Malachi 4:2

Journal

Journal

O God, with all my heart I thank you.

Dr. Joel Mattison worked with
missionary doctor Albert Schweitzer
in a clinic among the very poor in Africa.
He recalls the simple table grace
Schweitzer prayed before each meal:
"We thank the Lord for he is good,
and his loving kindness is forever."
Mattison said at a speech at Princeton,
"These were the words most frequently
overheard between him and God;
and when he died there at ninety,
they were certainly among his last."
The psalmist prays in a similar spirit.

Praise the LORD!
With all my heart I will thank the LORD
in the assembly of his people.
How wonderful are the things the LORD does!
All who are delighted with them
want to understand them.
All he does is full of honor and majesty. . . .
He is to be praised forever. 1–3, 10

How is it possible to be grateful to God
not only for the good things of life but
even more so for the trials God lets befall me?

For every hill I've had to climb . . .
For all the blood and sweat and grime . . .
My heart sings but a grateful song—
These were things that made me strong.
                                        Anonymous

O God, happy are they
who are generous to the needy.

The Sea of Galilee is alive and fresh.
The Dead Sea is brackish and salty. Both are fed
by the same water. Why the difference?
The Sea of Galilee gives up as much water
as it receives, spilling it into the Jordan.
The Dead Sea, on the other hand,
keeps every ounce of water that it receives,
losing only what the sun evaporates.
The two seas are images of the two kinds
of people in the world: "givers" and "keepers."
Psalm 112 talks about the givers.

Happy is the person who is generous . . . ,
who runs his business honestly. . . .
He will always be remembered. . . .
He gives generously to the needy,
and his kindness never fails. . . .
The wicked see this and are angry;
they glare in hate and disappear;
their hopes are gone forever. 4–6, 9–10

What are my thoughts as I speak to Jesus
about whether I resemble a giver or a keeper
and *listen* to his response?

A hundred times every day I remind myself
that my inner and outer life are based
on the labors of other men, living and dead,
and that I must exert myself in order to give
in the same measure as I have received
and am still receiving. Albert Einstein

*"The Kingdom of God
is within you."*
Luke 17:21

PRAYER PROCESS

*Every human being may be thought of
as being made up of four levels:
sense, mind, heart, and soul.
Each of these levels comes into play
in the meditation process.*

My *senses* come into play, primarily,
during the *reading* phase of meditation.
I try to discern what the people in the story
or the Scripture passage see, hear, feel.
My *mind* (conscious level) comes into play,
primarily, during the *thinking* phase
of meditation. I ponder some point
that struck me during the *reading* phase.

My *heart* (subconscious level) comes into play,
primarily, in the *speaking* phase.
I experience movements of my heart (joy, etc.)
and speak to Jesus about them.
My *soul* (sanctuary level) comes into play,
primarily, during the *listening* phase.
Jesus referred to this level when he said,
"The Kingdom of God is within you."
This is the level where Jesus speaks to me.

*This week I will try to be more sensitive
to the four levels and phases
that make up the meditation process.*

154

O God, from east to west your name is praised.

Psalms 113–118 are known as the *Hallel*, which derives from the Hebrew word *hallelujah* ("Praise the Lord"). Jesus and his disciples began the Last Supper singing Psalms 113–114 and concluded singing Psalms 115–118. Thus, Mark ends his Last Supper account, saying, "They sang . . . and went out to the Mount of Olives" (Mark 14:26).

Praise the LORD!
You servants of the LORD, praise his name!
May his name be praised, now and forever.
From the east to the west
praise the name of the LORD!
The LORD rules over all nations;
his glory is above the heavens.
There is no one like the LORD our God.
He lives in the heights above, but he bends down
to see the heavens and the earth.
He raises the poor from the dust;
he lifts the needy from their misery
and makes them companions of princes,
the princes of his people.
He honors the childless wife in her home;
he makes her happy by giving her children.
Praise the LORD! 1–9

For what ought I to praise my Lord?

"Be still, and know that I am God!"
Psalm 46:10 (NRSV)

Journal

Journal

O God, you made hills jump and the mountains skip.

"Moses held out his hand over the sea . . .
and the Israelites went through . . . ,
with walls of water on both sides"
(Exodus 14:21–22).
"The priests stepped into the river,
[and] the water stopped flowing and piled up"
(Joshua 3:15–16).
The crossings of the Red Sea
and the Jordan River are closely linked;
they are opposite sides of the same coin.
The crossing of the Red Sea marks
Israel's *exit* from a *land of slavery*.
The crossing of the Jordan River marks
Israel's *entry* into a *land of freedom*.
Psalm 114 celebrates these key events.

The Red Sea looked and ran away;
The Jordan River stopped flowing.
The mountains skipped like goats;
the hills jumped around like lambs.
What happened, Sea,
to make you run away?
And you, O Jordan,
why did you stop flowing?
You mountains, why did you skip like goats?
You hills, why did you jump?   3–6

What are two key events
in my personal journey to the Promised Land?

"I will be with you always."   Matthew 28:20

O God, you bless everyone who honors you.

The prophet Isaiah scorns idolatry:
"A person uses part of a tree for . . . a fire. . . .
He warms himself and says,
'How nice and warm!
What a beautiful fire!'
The rest of the wood he makes into an idol,
and then he bows down and worships it.
He prays to it and says, 'You are my god—
save me!' . . . It makes as much sense
as eating ashes."   Isaiah 44:15–17, 20
Likewise, the psalmist scorns idolatry:

Why should the nations ask us,
"Where is your God?"
Our God is in heaven;
he does whatever he wishes.
Their gods are . . . formed by human hands.
They have mouths, but cannot speak,
and eyes, but cannot see.
They have ears, but cannot hear. . . .
They have hands, but cannot feel,
and feet, but cannot walk. . . .
Trust in the LORD, you people of Israel. . . .
He will bless everyone who honors him,
the great and the small alike.   2–7, 9, 13

What are some idols in my life?

Put to death . . .
evil passions, and greed
(for greed is a form of idolatry).   Colossians 3:5

Journal

Journal

O God,
you saved me from death.

Mike Thomas was in his car,
approaching a dangerous, busy intersection.
Suddenly a blind couple,
tapping white canes and holding two infants,
stepped right into the path of his car.
He slammed on his brakes, just in time.
The couple became frightened
and began straying into the center
of the eight-lane intersection.
What happened next is hard to describe.
Every car in every lane screeched to a halt.
No horn sounded, no driver shouted.
The motorist next to Mike
stuck his head out of the window
and directed the couple to other side.
When they had crossed safely,
the traffic resumed its hectic, swift pace.

The danger of death was all around me; . . .
I was filled with fear and anxiety.
Then I called to the LORD. . . .
The LORD saved me from death. . . .
And so I walk in the presence of the LORD
in the world of the living. . . .
What can I offer the LORD
for all his goodness to me?   3–4, 8–9, 12

Can I recall a time the Lord helped me?
What can I offer the Lord for all his goodness?

No gift is mine until I've thanked the giver.

O God, your love is strong; your faithfulness is eternal.

If you're a trivia buff, you know Psalm 117
is the shortest psalm—only two verses.
But its message makes up for its brevity.
It capsulizes the content of the "good news"
that believers should preach to all peoples.
Martin Luther wrote:
"As I see it, the whole Book of Acts
was written because of this psalm."
For the Book of Acts is nothing more
than the story of God's people
responding to God's commission
to invite all nations to praise God.

Praise the LORD, all nations!
Praise him all peoples!
His love for us is strong,
and his faithfulness is eternal.
Praise the LORD!   1-2

How might I proclaim to others
the "good news" I have received?

"Everyone who calls out
to the Lord for help will be saved."
But how can they call to him for help if they
have not believed? And how can they believe
if they have not heard the message?
And how can they hear if the message
is not proclaimed? And how can the message
be proclaimed if the messengers
are not sent out?   Romans 10:13–15

O God, because of your love, I will not die, but live.

The Last Supper began with the singing
of the first half of the Hallel (Psalms 113–114)
and ended with the singing
of the last half (Psalms 115–118).
How prophetic Psalm 118
must have sounded to Jesus.

Give thanks to the LORD,
because he is good, and his love is eternal.
Let the people of Israel say,
"His love is eternal." . . .
I called to the LORD; he answered me. . . .
I will not be afraid. . . .
I will not die; instead, I will live
and proclaim what the LORD has done. . . .
The stone
which the builders rejected as worthless
turned out to be the most important of all.
This was done by the LORD;
what a wonderful sight it is!   1–2, 5–6, 17, 22–23

As I imagine myself walking with Jesus and
the apostles to Gethsemane after the Last Supper,
what are Jesus' thoughts? Mine?

[After Jesus' resurrection,
Peter told Jerusalem's religious leaders,]
"'The stone that you the builders despised
turned out to be the most important of all.'
Salvation is to be found through him alone."
Acts 4:11–12

Your word, O God, lights my path and guides me.

Journal

God's covenant at Mount Sinai changed Israel from a mob of slaves into God's chosen people. The Ten Commandments became God's guidelines for freeing the Israelites from selfishness and setting them on the road to love and service. Psalm 119 sums up Israel's attitude toward the commandments.

Happy are those who follow his commands,
who obey him with all their heart.
They never do wrong;
they walk in the LORD's ways. . . .
How I love your law!
I think about it all day long. . . .
Your word is a lamp to guide me
and a light for my path. . . .
I love your commands more than gold,
more than the finest gold. . . .
How certain your promise is! How I love it!
2–3, 97, 105, 127, 140

How do I account for Israel's attitude toward God's commandments?
How do I account for my attitude toward them?

[Jesus said,]
"I love you just as the Father loves me;
remain in my love. If you obey my commands,
you will remain in my love,
just as I have obeyed my Father's commands
and remain in his love."   John 15:9–10

Jesus . . .
looked up to heaven.
John 17:1

PRAYER CHECKUP

Spiritual directors suggest
that we do an occasional checkup
on what our body is doing during meditation.

Is my back erect?
A straight back cuts down distractions.
There is no scientific explanation for this,
but it is a common experience of meditators.
Are my eyes at rest?
One way to put them at rest is to close them
after the reading phase of meditation.
Another way is to focus them on a crucifix,
a burning candle, or a picture.
Are my hands at rest?

If not, I might try placing them palms up
on the arms of my "prayer chair."
Or I might rest my elbows on the arms
of the chair, extending my arms upward,
with hands open and fingertips extended.
Is my breathing relaxed?
If not, I might try setting up a relaxed,
rhythmic pattern of breathing.
Finally, is my body at rest?
The less it moves, the better I can pray.

This week I will run a ten-second body checkup
after each meditation.

O God, when I speak of peace, they are for war.

Father Paul Belliveau was the pastor
of a refugee camp in Honduras.
It was jammed with thousands of men,
women, and children who had fled
the brutal political situation in El Salvador.
Father Paul writes: "I saw many women
in the chapel praying. I entered and sat down.
About eighty women
were saying the Stations of the Cross.
Every station identified the suffering of Jesus
with the refugees.
They told me they called their group
'Mothers who have lost children
due to violence in El Salvador.' "
Psalm 120 expresses the feelings
of many of these refugee mothers.

Save me, LORD, from liars and deceivers.
You liars, what will God do to you?
How will he punish you? . . .
Living among you is as bad as living . . .
among the people of Kedar. I have lived
too long with people who hate peace!
When I speak of peace, they are for war. 2–3, 5–7

If I asked a mother in the chapel
how I could help her, what might she say?

Injustice anywhere
is a threat to justice everywhere.
Martin Luther King Jr.

Journal

O God, my help comes from you, who made heaven and earth.

James Irwin's voyage to the moon changed
his life forever.
He says in *To Rule the Night:*
"I wish I had been a writer or a poet,
so that I could convey more adequately
the feeling of this flight. . . .
The ultimate effect has been to deepen
and strengthen all the religious insight
I ever had. It has made my faith. . . .
On the moon the total picture of the power
of God and his Son Jesus Christ became abundantly
clear to me." Elsewhere he writes
that the moon's mountains, "at first sight,
were not gray or brown as I expected.
They were golden." He adds that as he gazed
at them the words of Psalm 121 kept echoing
in his mind "like the refrain of an old hymn."

I look to the mountains;
where will my help come from?
My help will come from the LORD,
who made heaven and earth.   1–2

Why do I think so many astronauts
had religious experiences in connection
with their space travel?

I sing the mighty power of God,
That made the mountains rise;
That spread the flowing seas abroad,
And built the lofty skies.   Isaac Watts (1715)

O God, how glad I am to be in your holy city.

On January 5, 1964, Pope Paul VI became
the first pope to visit Jerusalem during his reign
in office. Immediately upon entering
the walled city through Saint Stephen's gate,
the pope paused and prayed Psalm 122.

I was glad when they said to me,
"Let us go to the LORD's house."
And now we are here,
standing inside the gates of Jerusalem! . . .
This is where the tribes come, the tribes
of Israel, to give thanks to the LORD. . . .
Here the kings of Israel
sat to judge their people.
Pray for the peace of Jerusalem: . . .
"May there be peace inside your walls
and safety in your palaces."
For the sake of my relatives and friends
I say to Jerusalem, "Peace be with you!"
For the sake of the house of the LORD our God
I pray for your prosperity.   1–2, 4–9

What must Jesus have thought when,
as a young pilgrim of twelve,
he prayed Psalm 122 upon entering the city?

[Jesus said,] "Jerusalem, Jerusalem! . . .
How many times I wanted to put my arms
around all your people, just as a hen
gathers her chicks under her wings,
but you would not let me!"   Luke 13:34

Journal

Journal

Be merciful to me, O God, be merciful.

"When Chesterton was a schoolboy,
he wrote about a book he had read:
'What I like about this novelist is that he takes
such trouble about his minor characters.'
To the eye of faith
it is a matter of unceasing wonder, love,
and praise how the divine Author takes
such trouble about his minor characters,
human and other. As I have seen
written somewhere: 'Even the sparrow
is a cheeky little somebody to Him.' "
Carroll E. Simcox, *Learning to Believe*

LORD, I look up to you, up to heaven,
where you rule.
As a servant depends on his master,
as a maid depends on her mistress,
so we will keep looking to you,
O LORD our God,
until you have mercy on us.
Be merciful to us, LORD, be merciful;
we have been treated with so much contempt.
We have been mocked too long by the rich
and scorned by proud oppressors.   1–4

Why is a minor character like a sparrow
"a cheeky little somebody" to God?

God purposely chose
what the world considers nonsense
in order to shame the wise.   1 Corinthians 1:27

O God, we thank you for coming to our rescue.

Angelo Roncalli, the future Pope John XXIII,
was eating with his secretary.
The secretary was challenging
the cardinal's tolerance of a troublesome priest.
"Why not dismiss him?" After listening awhile,
the cardinal picked up his empty wine glass
and asked, "Whose glass is this?"
The secretary replied, "It's yours, of course."
Then the cardinal broke the glass and said,
"Now whose glass is it?"
The secretary said,
"Why, I guess I must say it is still yours."
The cardinal said, "Is that troublesome priest
any less my brother than the glass still is,
in spite of its brokenness?"
Psalm 124 recalls that God did not give up
on Israel either, in spite of its brokenness.

"If the LORD had not been on our side
when our enemies attacked us,
then they would have swallowed us. . . ."
Let us thank the LORD,
who has not let our enemies destroy us. . . .
Our help comes from the LORD,
who made heaven and earth.   2–3, 6, 8

Where would I be if God had given up on me
because of my own brokenness?

There is no saint without a past—
and no sinner without a future.   Anonymous

Journal

Journal

O God, I trust in you now and forever.

In *Ever Wonder Why?* Douglas Smith
cites the origin of the practice
of clinking glasses before drinking a toast.
He recalls that centuries ago
it was not all that uncommon for hosts
to give guests poisoned drinks.
To assure a guest the drink was not poisoned,
the host held out his glass to let his guest
pour some of his own drink into it.
If the guest wanted to show the host
that he trusted him, he declined
and simply clinked his host's glass with his.
It is in this spirit of trust in God
that the psalmist writes:

Those who trust in the LORD
are like Mount Zion,
which can never be shaken, never be moved.
As the mountains surround Jerusalem,
so the LORD surrounds his people,
now and forever.   1–2

How strong is my trust in God—
especially when life seems to turn against me?

Even though the fig trees have no fruit
and no grapes grow on the vines,
even though the olive crop fails
and the fields produce no grain, . . .
I will still be joyful and glad, because
the LORD God is my savior.   Habakkuk 3:17–18

O God, how we sang for joy when we returned home.

Journal

The crowd cheered wildly as a plane
filled with American POWs from Vietnam
hit the runway.
A similar cheer burst forth from the POWs
inside the plane as they taxied to a stop.
The joy that filled their hearts
was the same joy that filled the hearts
of Jewish POWs returning from Babylon
to Jerusalem in 538 B.C.E.
The first year back in Jerusalem, however,
the crops failed and they had to eat less
in order to have enough seed to plant.

When the LORD brought us back to Jerusalem,
it was like a dream!
How we laughed, how we sang for joy! . . .
Indeed he did great things for us;
how happy we were!
LORD, make us prosperous again. . . .
Let those who wept as they planted . . .
gather the harvest with joy!
Those who wept as they went out
carrying the seed will come back singing for joy,
as they bring in the harvest. 1–6

When have I felt the peace and the joy
that come from putting all my trust in God
when it seems impossible for me to trust?

Ah, if you knew what peace there is
in accepted sorrow. Madame Guyon

VII

The Psalms and Jesus

A house without any windows
would be like a face without any eyes.
What windows are to the world,
the psalms are to the Bible.
The psalms let us look out onto the landscape
of the biblical world.
More importantly,
they let us look into the hearts
of the people who walked around in it.
They let us see how these people felt
in moments of sorrow, joy, and danger.
Take just one example.

If we want to know
what went on in the heart and mind of Jesus
as he hung on the cross,
we could do no better than read Psalm 22.
Both Mark and Matthew describe Jesus
praying that psalm on that tragic occasion
(Mark 15:34, Matthew 27:46).

Written about six hundred years before
the Romans devised death by crucifixion,
Psalm 22 mirrors Jesus' situation perfectly.

My God, my God,
why have you abandoned me?. . .

My strength is gone,
gone like water spilled on the ground.
All my bones are out of joint;
my heart is like melted wax.
My throat is as dry as dust. . . .
O LORD, don't stay away from me!   1, 14–15, 19

And if we wanted to know
what went on in the mind of Jesus
as he made the yearly pilgrimage
from Nazareth to the Jerusalem Temple,
we could do no better than read Psalm 84.
This was one of the psalms pilgrims prayed
on their way to Mount Zion, the hill
on which the walled city of Jerusalem stood.

How I love your Temple. . . .
How I want to be there! . . .
With my whole being I sing for joy
to the living God. . . .
How happy are those whose strength
comes from you, who are eager
to make the pilgrimage to Mount Zion. . . .
They grow stronger as they go;
they will see the God of gods on Zion.   1–2, 5, 7

Journal

*"The spirit is willing,
but the flesh is weak."*
Matthew 26:41

PRAYER AND DISTRACTIONS

*Keith Miller was plagued by distractions.
His mind would flit from a phone call
he should make to a letter he should write.
A friend suggested he keep a notepad next to
his "prayer chair." When such thoughts came,
he should jot them down and go on praying.
He did this, and to his surprise
he found that a number of distractions
were things he should do.*

Miller's experience illustrates something
I need to keep in mind: God sometimes speaks
to me through my distractions—
things I should attend to.

Saint Francis de Sales puts a similar spin
on distractions. He says that distractions,
if handled properly, can enhance prayer.
When they occur, he says,
"Bring your wayward heart back home quietly.
If you did nothing else during prayer
but return your heart continually
and patiently to the Master's side,
your time of prayer would be well spent."

*This week, when distractions occur,
I will either jot them down or return
my "wayward heart" to its "Master's side."*

Without your help, O God, our work is useless.

The Constitutional Convention
was deadlocked in Philadelphia in 1787.
The colonies could not agree on a form
of central government. At this point,
eighty-one-year-old Benjamin Franklin said,
"If the LORD does not build the house,
the work of the builders is useless" (Psalm 127:1).
Then he moved that the delegates
begin the next day's meeting with prayer.
The deadlock was resolved, a nation was born,
and Congress still begins sessions with prayer.

If the LORD does not build the house,
the work of the builders is useless;
if the LORD does not protect the city,
it does no good for the sentries
to stand guard.
It is useless to work so hard for a living,
getting up early and going to bed late.
For the LORD provides for those he loves,
while they are asleep.   1–2

How do I express my need for God's help?

We come closest to God in our lowest moments.
It is easiest to hear God
when you are stripped of pride and arrogance,
when you have nothing to rely on except God.
It is painful to get to that point,
but when you do, God is there.
        Terry Anderson, five years as a hostage in Lebanon

Journal

O God, happy are they who live by your word.

Dr. Ed Tennant and his wife, June,
were childless for ten years.
Then on impulse, they accepted an infant
with foot deformities so severe
that they were told she would never walk.
That was the start of a foster family
that eventually increased
to twelve "unadoptable" children—
all needing corrective surgery.
Ed and June agree completely on one thing:
"These children have given us more
than we've given them."

Happy are those who obey the LORD,
who live by his commands.
Your work will provide for your needs;
you will be happy and prosperous.
Your wife will be like a fruitful vine
in your home, and your children will be
like young olive trees around your table.
A man who obeys the LORD
will surely be blessed like this. 1–4

What are some of the unanticipated blessings
God has given me?

The Disciple asked the Master,
"Where must the seed be sown
to bring the most fruit when it is grown?"
The Master replied, "Go plant it
in the heart of a child." Author unknown

O God, your love has set me free.

Israel's history is a history of suffering.
It began in Egypt under the whips
of cruel taskmasters. It continued
even after Israel entered the Promised Land.
But God's people weathered the storms
and outlasted their enemies. They compared
their foes to the grass that sprouted during
the rainy season on their mud-covered roofs.
When the sun appeared, the grass died.
Psalm 129 reviews Israel's history.

"Ever since I was young,
my enemies have persecuted me cruelly,
but they have not overcome me.
They cut deep wounds in my back
and made it like a plowed field.
But the LORD, the righteous one,
has freed me from slavery."
May everyone who hates Zion
be defeated and driven back.
May they all be like grass
growing on the housetops,
which dries up before it can grow.   2–6

What lesson might I draw
from the history of Israel?

This is Daddy's bedtime secret for today:
Man is born broken. He lives by mending.
The grace of God is glue.
      Eugene O'Neill, *The Great God Brown*

Journal

Journal

I trust in your word, O God, and wait for your help.

Columbus wrote in his journal
that as his ship sailed past La Rabida
the crew could hear the monks on land
chanting morning prayers.
As weeks passed, however, things changed.
None of Columbus's sailors had been more
than a few hundred miles from shore.
Now they were thousands of miles
and still going. Fear gripped the crew.
We can see Columbus alone in his cabin.
Staring down at the last entry in his journal,
"Still no land!" he begins to wonder,
"Have I failed?" Voyaging to God in prayer
is like that. A day comes when we may stare
at the wall discouraged and ask ourselves,
"Have I failed?" All we can do is
cry out to the Lord, trust in God,
and wait for the Lord to act.

I wait eagerly for the LORD's help,
and in his word I trust.
I wait for the LORD more eagerly
than sentries wait for the dawn—
than sentries wait for the dawn.   5–6

Why might God keep me waiting for such
a long time before answering my prayer?

Only those who can contain within themselves
the pressure and chaos of tension
can give birth to a dancing star.   Nietzsche

I gave up my pride, O God, and my heart grew peaceful.

Someone compared Psalm 131
to the ringing of a church bell
at that magic moment when the setting sun
arrays the world in a glow of gold.
This short psalm describes the heart
of the *ani* ("poor people") of Jesus' time.
Powerless and devoid of worldly means,
they had become *detached*
from the material things of this world
and totally *attached*
to God and the spiritual things
of the next world.
Jesus had these people in mind
when he said, "Happy are you poor;
the Kingdom of God is yours!" (Luke 6:20).

LORD, I have given up my pride
and turned away from my arrogance.
I am not concerned with great matters
or with subjects too difficult for me.
Instead, I am content and at peace.
As a child lies quietly in its mother's arms,
so my heart is quiet within me.   1–2

How detached am I from the material things
of this world, and how attached am I
to God's promises and spiritual things?

Do you want to know how rich you are?
Count the number of things you possess
that money can't buy.

Journal

177

You made a promise to David, O God, that will never end.

God's promise to David of an eternal kingship from his royal line began a series of promises that pointed to a person called the Messiah. The messianic promises reached their ultimate fulfillment in Jesus. Psalm 132 celebrates God's promise to David.

You made a promise to your servant David;
do not reject your chosen king, LORD.
You made a solemn promise to David—
a promise you will not take back:
"I will make one of your sons king,
and he will rule after you.
If your sons are true to my covenant
and to the commands I give them,
their sons, also, will succeed you
for all time as kings."
The LORD has chosen Zion;
he wants to make it his home:
"This is where I will live forever;
this is where I want to rule. . . .
Here I will make one of David's descendants
a great king; here I will preserve the rule
of my chosen king."   10–14, 17

What role do I think Jesus wants me to play in the kingdom of God?

The cost of being a disciple is big;
the cost of not being one is bigger still.
Author unknown

Journal

O God, how pleasant it is to live together in harmony.

Jerry Kramer describes his feelings after Green Bay won its third championship: "We rushed to the locker room . . . shouting and absolutely floating. . . . I felt so proud, proud of myself and proud of my teammates and proud of my coaches. . . .
I felt like I was part of something special. . . .
It's the feeling of being together, completely together, a singleness of purpose, accomplishing something a lot of people thought we couldn't accomplish. It sent a beautiful shiver up my back."
Instant Replay: The Green Bay Diary of Jerry Kramer
Psalm 133 celebrates a similar feeling.

How wonderful it is, how pleasant,
for God's people to live together in harmony!
It is like the precious anointing oil
running down from Aaron's head and beard,
down to the collar of his robes.
It is like the dew on Mount Hermon,
falling on the hills of Zion. That is where
the LORD has promised his blessing—
life that never ends.   1–3

Can I recall a similar feeling of joyful unity?

In Christ there is no East or West,
In him no South or North,
But one great fellowship of love
Throughout the whole wide earth.   Old hymn

Journal

179

[Jesus] threw himself
face downward on the ground and prayed.
Matthew 26:39

PRAYER AND FEELING

In his book The Taste of New Wine,
Keith Miller talks about a problem he had.
He did not always feel God's presence.
One day he shared his concern with a friend.
During the sharing, it dawned on Keith
that feeling was not the point of praying.
This gave him a new view of himself
and of his problem. He writes:
"So much of my life I had been . . . always
wanting to feel God's presence in my prayers
and being depressed when I didn't. . . .
So I tried praying . . . whether I felt spiritual
or not and found for the first time in my life
that we can live on raw faith. Moreover,

I found that often the very act of praying this way
brings later a closer sense of God's presence."

———————

I need to keep in mind Keith's last point:
The "grace of prayer" often comes outside
the time of prayer—later on.
In other words, seeds planted during prayer
often take time to germinate.

This week I will remember that prayer time
is often a seed-planting time, and I will not
become discouraged if nothing seems to be
happening during my time of prayer.

O God, bless those who serve you at night.

Journal

A TV "news-magazine" program
did a fascinating story on night workers
in downtown stores and office buildings.
They are the people who clean, maintain,
and guard these buildings during the night.
They work unheralded behind the scenes
to make these buildings function efficiently.
A similar group of people worked at similar jobs
in the Jerusalem Temple (1 Chronicles 9:26–34).
They cleaned, maintained, and
kept the Temple safe and secure.
Appropriately the tiny psalm that concludes
the series of "pilgrim psalms" takes the form
of a blessing on people who work
behind the scenes in the Jerusalem Temple.

Come, praise the LORD,
all his servants,
all who serve in his Temple at night.
Raise your hands in prayer in the Temple,
and praise the LORD!
May the LORD, who made heaven and earth,
bless you from Zion!   1–3

How often and contentedly do I give myself
to behind-the-scenes work?
What motivates me to do it?

The highest reward for a person's toil
is not what they get for it,
but what they become by it.   John Ruskin

O God, we praise you in your house.

God of the Oppressed by James Cone
has a beautiful description of worship
in the black community in early slave days:
"Through song, prayer, and sermon
the community affirmed Jesus' presence
and their willingness
to make it through a troubled situation.
Some would smile and others would cry.
Another person,
depending upon the Spirit's effect on him,
would clap his hands and tap his feet. . . .
All of these expressions were nothing
but black people bearing witness
to Jesus' presence among them."
Psalm 135 calls Israel to a similar worship.

Praise his name, you servants of the LORD,
who stand in the LORD's house. . . .
Praise the LORD, because he is good;
sing praises to his name,
because he is kind. . . .
The LORD will defend his people;
he will take pity on his servants. . . .
Praise the LORD . . . in Jerusalem, his home.
Praise the LORD!   1–3, 14, 21

Can I recall a memorable worship experience?

Great . . . are they
who see that the spiritual is stronger
than any material force.   Ralph Waldo Emerson

Journal

O God, we thank you, for your love is eternal.

Journal

Dorothy Day was a champion of justice for the poor. Among her many traits one stood out: her sense of gratitude. Her close associate, Eileen Egan, cites an example:
"We were in a boat going down the Thames. It was cold, and she was wearing only a thin coat. She had a copy of The London Times with her, so she wrapped the sheets of newspaper around her under the coat and said:
'I thank the men on the Bowery for teaching me this way of keeping warm.' Wherever we were, she found a reason to be thankful." *America* magazine (2/10/96)
No doubt Psalm 136 had a special niche in the great heart of Dorothy Day.

Give thanks to the LORD, because he is good;
his love is eternal.
Give thanks to the greatest of all gods;
his love is eternal.
Give thanks to the mightiest of all lords;
his love is eternal. . . .
Give thanks to the God of heaven;
his love is eternal.   1–3, 26

Can I always find a reason to be thankful?

On her grave stone in the cemetery of the Resurrection on Staten Island, she [Dorothy] wanted only two words to be inscribed:
Deo Gratias *("Thanks be to God").*   Eileen Egan

Journal

_____
_____
_____
_____
_____
_____
_____
_____
_____
_____
_____
_____

O God, let me never forget your holy city.

Judah's "day of drums" dawned in 586 B.C.E.
Babylonian armies invaded and destroyed
the city of Jerusalem and the Temple.
Jews skilled in arts and crafts
were led off to Babylon.
Some of these Jews drifted from their faith.
Others underwent a profound conversion;
they lived only for the day when they could
return to Jerusalem and rebuild the Temple.
Psalm 137 captures their deepest feelings
in these unforgettable words:

By the rivers of Babylon we sat down;
there we wept when we remembered Zion.
On the willows near by we hung up our harps.
Those who captured us told us to sing;
they told us to entertain them: "Sing us a song
about Zion." How can we sing a song
to the LORD in a foreign land?
May I never be able to play the harp again
if I forget you, Jerusalem! May I never be able
to sing again . . . if I do not think of you
as my greatest joy!   1–6

What impact do trials have on my faith
and my own peace of mind?

Happy are those who remain faithful
under trials, because . . . they will receive as
their reward the life which God has promised
to those who love him.   James 1:12

O God, I thank you with all my heart.

Twenty years ago, Tony Williams
was paralyzed from the chest down.
A sniper shot him randomly as he walked home
after a playground basketball game.
Today Tony gives talks to young people
with physical disabilities like his.
Recently he said, "You know, with gangs
in my old neighborhood in Chicago—
I don't know how to say this—
but it's possible
that I would have been worse off
if I hadn't gotten shot that day. . . .
When you have a lot of pain in your life,
the pain changes things.
In my case, it brought me closer to God;
and my faith has helped my life
to be a very happy life."

I thank you, LORD, with all my heart . . .
and praise your name because of your
constant love and faithfulness. . . .
You answered me when I called to you;
with your strength you strengthened me. . . .
Even though you are so high above,
you care for the lowly. . . .
LORD, your love is eternal.   1–3, 6, 8

What message does Tony's faith have for me?

Sorrow looks back, worry looks around,
faith looks up.   Anonymous

Journal

Psalm 139 Day six

Journal

_____

O God, you are around me on every side.

During World War II, Eddie Rickenbacker and a crew of seven crashed into the Pacific. For twenty-one days they floated on rubber life rafts. All supplies were lost in the crash, except for four small oranges. After eight days it rained and the men were able to collect water to drink. On another occasion a seagull landed on Rick's head. He caught it for food, which the men shared. After twenty-one days, rescue came. Seven of the eight men were still alive. One of the things that kept them going was a prayer session each day. And one of the most popular prayers at these sessions was Psalm 139.

LORD, you have examined me and you know me.
You know everything I do; from far away
you understand all my thoughts.
You see me, whether I am working or resting;
you know all my actions.
Even before I speak, you already know
what I will say.
You are all around me on every side;
you protect me with your power.
Your knowledge of me is too deep;
it is beyond my understanding.   1–6

Why would Psalm 139 prove so popular?

When they are in trouble,
I will be with them.   Psalm 91:15

O God, you are my God, and I live in your presence.

Journal

"[To be a child] is to have a spirit
yet streaming with the waters of baptism;
it is to believe in love, . . . it is to be
so little that the elves can reach
to whisper in your ear;
it is to turn pumpkins into coaches,
and mice into horses, lowness into loftiness,
and nothing into everything, for each child
has a fairy godmother in its own soul;
it is to live in a nutshell and count yourself
the king of infinite space; it is
> To see a world in grain of sand,
> And a Heaven in a wild flower,
> Hold infinity in the palm of your hand,
> And eternity in an hour;
it is to know not as yet that you are under
sentence of life, nor petition that it be
commuted into death." Francis Thompson,
"Shelly," *The Works of Francis Thompson*, vol. 3 (1913)

*I say to the LORD, "You are my God." . . .
LORD, I know that you defend the cause
of the poor and the rights of the needy.
The righteous will praise you indeed;
they will live in your presence.* 6, 12–13

When am I like a child?

*Every time a child says, "I don't believe
in fairies," there is a little fairie somewhere
that falls down dead.* James Barrie

In great anguish
[Jesus] prayed even more fervently.
Luke 22:44

PRAYER AND DRYNESS

Sometimes people suddenly begin
to experience difficulty praying.
They wonder what they are doing wrong.
Just the opposite may be true.

I need to keep in mind that an experience
of dryness in prayer may be a sign of growth
in prayer. A man comments on his experience
of dryness: "At first, I was alarmed.
Then I recalled the corn-planting season as a boy
in Wisconsin. The first thing we did
was to pray for rain. The rain came down;
the corn came up. It was so beautiful we wanted
to dance. Then we did something strange!

We prayed for a period of dryness.
We did this because too much rain causes
the roots of corn to go out laterally
and keeps the tap root from searching for water.
If this happened, the crop would be inferior.
God does something similar with us.
At first meditation is exciting. But then God
sometimes gives us a period of dryness
to force our tap root to go through
the *feeling* level down to the *faith* level
in order to bear better fruit."   Joe Cramblit

This week I will recall that dryness in prayer
may be a sure sign that God is at work in me.

I call on you, O God;
help me now.

Saint Francis of Assisi was born in 1182
to a wealthy Italian family.
As a teenager he was a playboy.
At the age of twenty he joined the army,
was captured, and spent a year in prison.
After his release he returned home,
turned his back on his family's wealth,
and began to preach the Gospel on street corners.
Young people, especially, flocked to join
the charismatic Francis in his work.
At the age of twenty-seven he founded
a religious order that thrives to this day.
On October 3, 1226, at the age of forty-four,
Francis died lying on the bare ground
and praying Psalm 141.

I call to you, LORD;
help me now!
Listen to me when I call to you.
Receive my prayer as incense,
my uplifted hands
as an evening sacrifice.   1–2

If I had my choice, what would I pick
as a place and a prayer for departing life?

[LORD,] a thousand years to you . . .
are like yesterday, already gone,
like a short hour in the night. . . .
Teach us how short our life is,
so that we may become wise.   Psalm 90:4, 12

Journal

No one cares for me, O God; I cry to you for help.

Paul Kordenbrock is a prisoner on Death Row
in the Kentucky State Penitentiary.
He underwent a remarkable conversion
and has helped several prisoners to find Christ.
An appeal to have his case reviewed
was turned down. Shortly afterward he wrote:
"At times being a Christian seems easy. . . .
You feel as if Christ would be well pleased
with your life and how you are living for him.
There are also times when nothing you think,
do, or say feels right. . . . You catch yourself
wondering if it is even possible to be a follower
of Christ." Paul is the kind of person
who finds it easy to relate to the feelings
of the person in Psalm 142.

There is no one to help me,
no one to protect me. No one cares for me.
LORD, I cry to you for help;
you, LORD, are my protector;
you are all I want in this life.
Listen to my cry for help,
for I am sunk in despair.
Save me from my enemies;
they are too strong for me. 4–6

What do I say to Jesus about people like Paul?
What do I say to people like Paul about Jesus?

Tears may flow in the night,
but joy comes in the morning. Psalm 30:5

Like dry ground, O God, my soul is thirsty for you.

Time magazine described the prison status of a priest arrested in Rumania during the days of Communism. He was kept in a basement next to an open cesspool in total darkness. His bed was two boards on a damp floor. Rats ran over him at night. He writes: "I passed unforgettable moments of intimate union with the crucifix, which I conjured up before my mind. . . . There is a part of the living God which is only known to those who are themselves hidden in some subterranean cell, in darkness and in chains." Psalm 143 describes his situation.

My enemies have hunted me down
and completely defeated me.
They have put me in a dark prison,
and I am like those who died long ago.
So I am ready to give up. . . .
I think about all that you have done,
I bring to mind all your deeds.
I lift up my hands to you in prayer;
like dry ground my soul is thirsty for you.   3–6

What are my thoughts as I imagine myself to be the priest at the end of a month, with no idea of how long this will last?

God's happiness rests longer upon those
who have not light's distraction.
Rumanian priest-prisoner

Journal

O God, who are we that you pay attention to us?

The starting point for meditation
is the realization of the tremendous contrast
between God's infinite greatness
and our finite smallness.
Furthermore, this realization
invites us to marvel even more so
at the fact that this great God created us,
holds us in existence, and
wants to protect us from all spiritual evil—
so that we may enjoy God's presence forever.
The psalmist alludes to all this in Psalm 144.

Praise the LORD, my protector . . .
and defender, my shelter and savior. . . .
LORD, what are mortals,
that you notice them;
mere mortals, that you pay attention to us?
We are like a puff of wind;
our days are like a passing shadow. . . .
Reach down from above,
pull me out of the deep water, and rescue me. . . .
I will sing you a new song, O God;
I will play the harp and sing to you. . . .
Happy are the people whose God is the LORD!
1–4, 7, 9, 15

For what, especially, do I feel a need
for God's help and protection?

Where the human spirit fails,
the Holy Spirit fills.   Anonymous

O God, you are near to those who call upon you.

Daddy entered the kitchen without greeting
little Jennifer, who was eating her cereal.
She grabbed his arm, kissed him, and said,
"Daddy, you forgot to say hello!"
Daddy hugged her and said, "Sorry, Jenny!
I didn't notice you. I was thinking about
a problem that I must deal with today."
Jennifer said, "Did you say your prayers yet?"
"No," he said. "Come with me!" she said,
leading him to her prayer corner in her room.
Closing her eyes, she paused momentarily.
Then she said in a soft voice: "Jesus said,
"Don't be afraid, I am always with you."
After another pause, she looked up and said,
"Daddy, think about that a minute
and you'll feel much better."
They hugged and both went on their ways.
Retold from François Darcy-Berube

The LORD is loving and merciful. . . .
He is near to those who call to him. . . .
He supplies the needs of those who honor him;
he hears their cries and saves them.
He protects everyone who loves him. . . .
I will always praise the LORD.   8, 18–21

What might I do to help children discover Jesus
as Jennifer discovered him?

It is easier for parents to have children than
for children to have parents.   John XXIII (adapted)

Journal

Journal

I will praise you, O God, as long as I live.

Osborne Jera was startled to hear someone
singing at the top of his voice
in an empty church in the middle of the day.
Looking around, he saw a man,
hat in hand, eyes closed, facing the altar.
When his song ended,
the man opened his eyes.
Seeing Jera, he explained, "I just felt
like singing to God—if he's still here.
Such awful things happenin' in the world.
Felt like a little song might cheer him up."
Then the man flashed empty hands, saying,
"I haven't touched anything." Jera thought,
"How wondrously wrong he was to say
'I haven't touched anything!'"

Praise the LORD! . . .
I will praise him as long as I live;
I will sing to my God all my life. . . .
Happy are those . . .
who depend on the LORD their God,
the Creator of heaven, earth, and sea,
and all that is in them. . . .
Praise the LORD! 1–2, 5–6, 10

How do I interpret Jera's words,
"How wondrously wrong he was to say,
'I haven't touched anything!'"

What comes from the heart
touches the heart. Don Sibet

You number the stars, O God, and call each by name.

There comes a time in most of our lives
when we glimpse for a split moment
into the greatness and the glory of God—
often in nature.
Here is a description of such an experience:
"The vault of heaven, full of soft, shining
stars, stretched vast and fathomless. . . .
Alyosha stood and gazed, and
suddenly threw himself down on the earth.
He did not know why he embraced it. . . .
But he kissed it, weeping. . . .
Something firm and unshakable
as that vault of heaven
had entered his soul. . . .
And never, never, all his life long,
could Alyosha forget that minute."
Feodor Dostoevski, *The Brothers Karamazov*
Psalm 146 describes a similar moment.

Praise the LORD! . . .
He has decided the number of the stars
and calls each one by name.
Great and mighty is our Lord;
his wisdom cannot be measured. . . .
Praise the LORD! 1, 4–5, 20

What is the closest thing I have had
to a glimpse into God's greatness and glory?

It is the heart that experiences God,
not the reason. Blaise Pascal

*"When you pray,
do not use
a lot of meaningless words."*
Matthew 6:7

PRAYER AND MOTIVATION

*People meditate and pray for many reasons.
For example, it gives them peace of mind;
it gives them insight into problems;
it gives strength in times of trouble;
it gives courage in time of fear.
Last but not least, God answers prayers:
"Ask, and you will receive"* (Luke 11:9).
*These are splendid reasons for praying.
But they are secondary to the main reason.*

I must always keep in mind that prayer
and meditation are not an end in themselves.
They are expressions of love to God,
who is love. Peter van Breeman hastens to add,
however, that this does not mean
that prayer has no useful effects.
It simply means that "usefulness"
cannot be the sole purpose of prayer.
For example,
a friendship offers many "useful" benefits,
but if they are the sole purpose for the friendship,
then there is no friendship at all.

*This week I will strive
to become more aware of meditation
as being an expression of love to God,
who is love.*

O God, the entire universe praises your name.

Apollo 13 lifted off Cape Kennedy on April 11, 1970, for a scheduled third moon trip.
On April 13, an oxygen leak forced astronauts Lovell, Swigert, and Haise to abandon ship and attempt a return to earth in the lunar module. As the spaceship swung around the moon, for what would be one of the most memorable voyages in space history, Lovell put his thumb to the window and covered the earth with it. He said later, "I could put everything I knew behind my thumb. . . . It gives me a humble feeling of how insignificant we really are in our solar system." Psalm 148 is a call for the solar system and all of creation to praise God.

Praise the LORD from heaven. . . .
Praise him, sun and moon;
praise him, shining stars.
Praise him, highest heavens. . . .
Praise the LORD from the earth. . . .
Praise him, hills and mountains. . . .
Let them all praise the name of the LORD!
1, 3–4, 7, 9, 13

What feelings of humility
does the solar system evoke in me?

O tell of his might, O sing of his grace;
Whose robe is the light, whose canopy space.
                              Robert C. Grant (d. 1838)

Journal

We praise you, O God, with dancing and song.

Antal Dorati, a former conductor
of Washington's National Symphony Orchestra,
was being interviewed.
The subject turned to dance—ballet.
Mr. Dorati surprised a few people
when he said that he believed that dance
in its finest form was an act of praise.
"I imagine," he said, "that the first dance
was a movement of adoration . . .
to give thanks to the creator."
Psalm 149 is one of several examples to show
the psalmist felt the same way about dance.

Praise the LORD!
Sing a new song to the LORD; praise him
in the assembly of his faithful people!
Be glad, Israel, because of your Creator;
rejoice, people of Zion, because of your king!
Praise his name with dancing;
play drums and harps in praise of him.
The LORD takes pleasure in his people. . . .
Let God's people . . . sing joyfully
all night long.   1–5

Why do/don't I believe that dancing
is an appropriate act of worship?

What the American poet and musician
Sidney Lanier said of music
is true also of dance and other art forms.
Ultimately, it is "love in search of a word."

O God, every living creature on earth praises your name.

Journal

Handel's *Messiah* opened in London,
with the king and the queen present.
As the performance swelled to a climax
and the "Hallelujah Chorus" was intoned,
the king was so moved
that he rose reverently to his feet
and stood the remaining time.
The audience followed suit—
a practice that continues to this very day.
Psalm 150 seems to have had a similar impact
on the people of Israel.
A finale to worship, it can be read in seconds
but probably took an hour to perform.
A conductor coordinated the whole,
signaling when each group was to come in.

Praise the LORD! . . .
Praise him with trumpets.
Praise him with harps and lyres.
Praise him with drums and dancing.
Praise him with harps and flutes.
Praise him with cymbals.
Praise him with loud cymbals.
Praise the LORD, all living creatures!
Praise the LORD!   1, 3–6

What are my thoughts as I close my eyes
and imagine the people praising God?

O Lord my God, . . . how great thou art!
how great thou art!   Stuart K. Hine

Books by Mark Link

Join the thousands who have found in Mark Link enriching new ways for daily prayer.

Vision 2000

Mission 2000

Action 2000

Challenge 2000

Bible 2000

Spirit 2000

Lent 2000

Advent/Christmas 2000